It's About Time

Authors
Linda Fawcett
Carol Gossett
Myrna Mitchell

Illustrator
Reneé Mason

Editors
Betty Cordel
Michelle Pauls

Desktop Publisher
Tracey Lieder

It's About Time

This book contains materials developed by the AIMS Education Foundation. **AIMS** (**A**ctivities **I**ntegrating **M**athematics and **S**cience) began in 1981 with a grant from the National Science Foundation. The non-profit AIMS Education Foundation publishes hands-on instructional materials (books and the monthly magazine) that integrate curricular disciplines such as mathematics, science, language arts, and social studies. The Foundation sponsors a national program of professional development through which educators may gain both an understanding of the AIMS philosophy and expertise in teaching by integrated, hands-on methods.

ISBN 1-881431-97-5
Printed in the United States of America

I Hear
and I
Forget,

I See and
I Remember,

I Do
and I
Understand.

Chinese Proverb

iii

It's About Time

It's About Time
Concepts and Skills

Developing a Sense of Time
The Long and Short of It
identifying *long time* and *short time*

Ordering Events
Before and After
identifying *before* and *after*
Line Up the Time
ordering events in the school day

Quantifying Time
Time Counts
timing by counting swings of a pendulum
Time in a Bottle!
timing with a sand timer

Developing an Awareness of Clocks
Clocks, Clocks, and More Clocks
comparing and contrasting a variety of clocks and watches

Reading an Analog Clock
Hour by Hour
developing an awareness of the clock as a number line
Hands on the Hour
exploring the concepts of time
Time by Fives
identifying minutes after the hour in five-minute intervals human circle clock
Double Time
identifying minutes after the hour in five-minute intervals, one handed analog clock
Name that Time
constructing and reading analog clocks with minute and hour hands, human clock in five-minute intervals
Two Timers
reading an analog clock on the hour and half hour, hidden number clock
Minute by Minute
constructing and reading analog clocks with minute and hour hands, human clock in one-minute intervals
How Time Flies
connecting the movement of the minute hand and the hour hand, minute intervals, using commercial clock

Reading a Digital Clock
Can You Tell Time?
reading a digital clock
Flipping Over Time
establishing relationships between digital and analog clocks

Elapsed Time
Watch the Time Fly
determining elapsed time
Time Matters
applying time to everyday events

Playful and Intelligent Practice
Triple Time
Time Travels
Who Has? Time
Time Out

It's About Time
An Overview of Time

NCTM Standards 2000*

Understand measurable attributes of objects and the units, systems, and processes of measurement

- *Recognize the attributes of length, volume, weight, area, and time*
- *Compare and order objects according to these attributes*
- *Understand how to measure using nonstandard and standard units*
- *Select an appropriate unit and tool for the attribute being measured*

Apply appropriate techniques, tools, and formulas to determine measurements

- *Use tools to measure*
- *Develop common referents for measures to make comparisons and estimates*

* Reprinted with permission from *Principles and Standards for School Mathematics,* 2000 by the National Council of Teachers of Mathematics. All rights reserved.

Building a Sense of Time

Children need experiences that allow them to explore concepts of time and develop ways to measure it. Students must recognize and develop a sense of the intervals of time between events. They need to understand the relative duration of events such as short time vs. long time. The emphasis at first and second grade should be on developing concepts of time as well as the mechanics of using an analog and digital clock. It is expected that by the end of third grade, students should be able to tell time to the nearest minute. This expectation requires first and second grade teachers to engage students in meaningful experiences that develop a conceptual understanding of time.

Measuring Time

Time can be thought of as the duration of an event. Like other attributes, such as length and weight, time is measured using a repeated unit. These units can be informal (the beat of a metronome, the steady drip of a leaky faucet), or they can be formal (seconds, minutes, hours, day). It is important for students to understand that timing an event requires them to begin timing at the start of the event and stop timing at the end of the event, whether they are using formal or informal units. Young children enjoy timing events with informal units as well as formal units.

Clock Reading

Learning to read a digital or analog clock is a skill. It has very little to do with the conceptual understanding of time. The skills of clock reading are related to the skills of reading any numbered scale. Students must first identify the scale the clock is displaying. The normal sequence followed in learning to read a clock is first to read clocks to the hour, then the half and quarter hours, and finally to five- and one-minute intervals.

The Language of Time

Time order words are a part of the students' real world. Later, tomorrow, and yesterday are used in conversations with young learners but often with little meaning. We need to engage students in activities that make use of these words in real contexts. Time order words can generally be grouped into three categories or time frames: the past (yesterday, before, etc.), the present (today, now, etc.), and the future (tomorrow, later, etc.). A list of vocabulary words and literature titles have been provided for use during your study of time.

Suggested Vocabulary

Tomorrow, today, yesterday, earlier, later, analog, digital, before, after, long hand, short hand, sundial, time zones, midnight, cuckoo, pendulum, morning, noon (meridiem), night, day, clock, watch, measurement, grandfather clock, A.M. (ante meridiem), P.M. (post meridiem), quarter-past, half-past, half-hour, hour, minute, interval, duration, long, short, dusk, dawn, clockwise, counterclockwise

Suggested Uses for the Vocabulary

- Write the word *time* on a chart and ask your students to generate as many words as they can that are related to time.
- Select words that would allow your students to classify them into past, present, and future categories.
- Allow students to make a picture dictionary that would include several of the words.
- Create individual time lines with the words today, yesterday, and tomorrow. To do this, have the students write about or draw something they did yesterday, something they did or will do today, and something they will do tomorrow, and sequence the events.
- Word of the day: Introduce one word each day, give the definition, and work together as a class to use the word in a sentence.
- Choose one word from the list each day and introduce it as a mystery word. Give four clues about the word and allow the children to guess what the word is.

time

later	today
before	now
after	yesterday
midnight	tomorrow
noon	soon
night	lunch
day	dinner
	breakfast
	earlier

Children's Literature for Time

Appelt, Kathi. *Bats Around the Clock.* HarperCollins. New York. 2000.

Axelrod, Amy. *Pigs on a Blanket.* Simon & Schuster. New York, 1996.

Bowers, Kathleen. *At This Very Minute.* Philomel Books. Boston. 1983.

Carle, Eric. *Grouchy Ladybug.* HarperCollins. New York. 1996

Davies, Kay. *Time and Clocks.* Thomson Learning. New York. 1993.

Gibbons, Gail. *Clocks and How They Go.* T.Y. Crowell. New York. 1979.

Glover, David. *Make It Work.* World Book. Chicago. 1996.

Gordon, Sharon. *Tick Tock Clock.* Troll Associates. Mahwah, N.J. 1982.

Harper, Dan. *Telling Time with Big Mama Cat.* Harcourt. Orlando. 1998.

Hutchins, Pat. *Clocks and More Clocks.* Aladdin. New York. 1994.

Katz, Bobbi. *Tick-tock, Let's Read the Clock.* Random House. Westminster, MD. 1988.

Llewellyn, Claire. *My First Book of Time.* Dorling Kindersley. Boston. 1992.

Murphy, Stuart. *Get up and Go!* HarperCollins. New York. 1996.

Neasi, Barbara. *Minute Is a Minute.* Children's Press. Chicago. 1988.

Singer, Marilyn. *Nine O'Clock Lullaby.* HarperCollins. New York. 1991.

Older, Jules. *Telling Time: How to Tell Time on Analog and Digital Clocks.* Charlesbridge
　　Publishing. Watertown, MA. 2000.

Pluckrose, Henry. *Time.* Children's Press. Chicago. 1995.

Slater, Teddy. *Just A Minute.* Scholastic, Inc. New York. 1996.

Ward, Cindy. *Cookies Week.* Scholastic, Inc. New York. 1988.

Williams, Rozanne. *The Time Song.* Creative Teaching Press. Cypress, CA. 1995.

Williams, Rozanne. *What Time Is It?* Creative Teaching Press. Cypress, CA. 1995.

Zubrowski, Bernie. *Clocks. Building and Experimenting* (Boston Children's Museum
　　Activity Book.) William Morrow & Company. New York. 1988.

Developing a Sense of Time

It is important to provide experiences that will help students develop a sense of time. They need to understand time duration. Students should observe the duration of certain events and compare them in terms of taking long or short periods of time. They need to understand that time duration can be dependent on personal perspective. What may seem like a short duration of time for an adult could be a very long duration for a student. Waiting ten more minutes to go to recess could seem like an "eternity" to a student.

Students need to gain an understanding of the passage of time. Seasonal passages as well as daily passages, night and day, all contribute to a better understanding of time.

The following activity engages students in identifying long and short durations of time, and sorting tasks based on the amount of time they take to complete.

Materials for this section:
- *Long Time/Short Time* picture collection
- *Long Time/ Short Time* chart labels
- Pocket chart
- 8 ½" x 11" paper, one per student

1

The Long and Short of It

Topic
Time intervals—duration

Key Question
How long does it take to complete these events?

Learning Goal
Students will classify events based on the time it takes to complete them.

Guiding Document
NCTM Standards 2000*
- *Recognize the attributes of length, volume, weight, area, and time*
- *Compare and order objects according to these attributes*
- *Develop common referents for measures to make comparisons and estimates*

Math
Measurement
    time

Integrated Processes
Observing
Comparing and contrasting
Classifying

Materials
For the class:
    picture cards (see *Management 1*)
    Long Period of Time/Short Period of Time chart
    pocket chart (see *Management 2*)

For each group:
    student sorting mats (see *Management 4*)
    picture collection

Management
1. Use the pictures included in this lesson. If more are needed, cut pictures from magazines or catalogs that depict events in daily life.
2. Using a pocket chart, make a two-section sorting chart. Label one section *Long Period of Time* and the other section *Short Period of Time.*
3. Place students into groups of two while working on this activity.
4. Each group will need to make a sorting mat by folding an $8\frac{1}{2}$" x 11" piece of paper in half lengthwise and labeling one side *Long Time* and the other *Short Time.*

Procedure
1. Distribute a set of picture cards to each group.
2. Direct one partner to select a picture card and act out the event pictured.
3. Tell each student group to place the card on the sorting mat under the heading that describes the amount of time it takes to perform the event. Ask the students to continue selecting cards in turn, acting out events, and sorting them on the chart.
4. Direct the students' attention to the sorting chart you prepared in the pocket chart. Hold up a picture card. Ask the students where they placed this event.
5. Continue this process with the other picture cards. If groups disagree about where an event should be placed, allow them to show how they acted out the event. Discuss how some events could take a long or short time.
6. Have each child draw a picture of something he/she does at home or school.
7. Invite the students to sort the pictures in the *Long Period of Time/Short Period of Time* chart.

Discussion
1. What are some things that take a long time to do? ...a short time to do? Does everyone agree? Why or why not?
2. Does it take you longer to wash your hands or give your dog a bath?
3. Why do you think recess seems so short?
4. Does it take longer to eat an apple or eat a whole meal?
5. Why is it important to know how long something takes?

Evidence of Learning
Listen as students justify why they placed the picture cards in the columns they did.

Extension
Send a magazine home and have each child cut out and bring back a picture of something that takes a long time to complete and another picture of something that takes a short time to complete.

The Long and Short of It

Picture Cards

The Long and Short of It

Picture Cards

Ordering Events

Students need to develop a sense of sequential order as it relates to time. Opportunities should be provided that will allow them to place events in time order. Time order words are another important aspect in ordering events for students. *Before*, *after*, *earlier*, and *later* are used frequently in our conversations with students, but they often mean little, if anything, to the students. Students must make use of these words in context. The two activities found in this section engage students in ordering their day as well as sequencing events based on picture clues.

Materials for this section:
- *Before and After* picture collection
- Overhead transparency
- Sets of sequence cards
- String
- Clothespins
- 3 x 5-inch cards
- *Before/After* spinner
- One paper fastener
- Sentence strips, one per student
- *Event Cards*

Before and After

Topic
Time sequence

Key Question
Why does the sequence of a set of events matter?

Learning Goals
Students will:
1. develop a sequence based on a benchmark event, and
2. tell a story based on a sequence of cards.

Guiding Document
NCTM Standards 2000*
- *Recognize the attributes of length, volume, weight, area, and time*
- *Compare and order objects according to these attributes*
- *Develop common referents for measures to make comparisons and estimates*

Math
Measurement
   time

Integrated Processes
Observing
Comparing and contrasting
Classifying

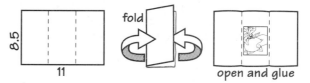

Materials
Picture collection (see *Management 1*)
Transparency of the birthday cake (see *Management 2*)
Sets of three sequence cards (see *Management 3*)
8 $\frac{1}{2}$" x 11" piece of paper, one per student

Management
1. Use the pictures provided or a similar collection of pictures depicting events in daily life cut out of magazines. Sets of comic strip pictures will be needed in *Part Three* of this activity. It is suggested that you limit the number of frames to no more than three and that you take the reading ability of your students into consideration when choosing these comic strips. Due to the difficulty of this task it may not be as important for the students to find the correct sequence as it is for them to sequence the pictures and tell the story of the ordered events.
2. Make a transparency of the birthday cake card. For better viewing, the picture can be enlarged prior to making the transparency.

3. Prepare enough sets of the three sequence cards so that each child will have a card for *Part One* of the activity.

Procedure
Part One
1. Place the transparency of the cake on the overhead. Have students describe the picture.
2. Ask the students to identify an action/event that would come before the picture of the cake and one that would come after. Invite the students to draw a picture of both. Make the connection of the words *before* and *after* to other vocabulary such as *earlier, later, yesterday, today, tomorrow,* etc.
3. Ask the students to sequence the three pictures. Be sure to check that the students have placed the cake in the middle without you telling them to.
4. Give each group of students an 8 $\frac{1}{2}$" x 11" sheet of paper. Assist the students in folding their paper into thirds.

	fold	
8.5		open and glue
11		

5. Distribute one or two cards from one of the sets of three sequence cards to each student. Instruct them to look at the picture or pictures that they were given and to think about what may have come before, after, or in between the picture or pictures that they received.
6. When the students have determined which piece or pieces of their sequence/story they have and which are missing, ask them to glue their picture or pictures onto the sheet of paper. Instruct them to place only one picture in each section, leaving a blank or blanks where necessary so that they can complete their sequence/story. For example, if they feel that they have the middle piece of the sequence, instruct them to glue that piece to the center section of the divided paper. Tell the students to draw in the pictures to complete the sequence/story. Allow them to share their work with the group by explaining what is taking place in their sequence of pictures.

Part Two
1. Tell the students that they will be playing a game that will help them practice sequencing events. Explain that in this activity, *sequencing* means to put events in the order that they happen.

2. Distribute a card to each child. Tell the students they must find the two matches to their card to make a sequence. Explain that there may be more than one set of the birthday sequence cards, tomato sequence cards, etc. so students may find a person holding a card that would match their set but that child is already part of another group. Allow the children time to walk around the room and compare their cards and find the ones that complete their sequences.
3. Have the students use the cards to write or tell a story that would match the sequence shown. Tell the students that the beginning of the story will come from the first picture, the middle of the story will come from the second picture, and the end will come from the last picture in the sequence.

Part Three
1. Remind the students of their prior experiences with sequencing and discuss with them places that they may see pictures of events in a sequence. [comic strips]
2. Tell the students that they will have a chance to sequence events in comic strips. Distribute one comic strip that has been cut apart and is out of sequence to each group of two students. Ask each group to sequence the events in the comic strip and then share their story with the class.

Discussion
1. Describe something you do each day that is before you eat lunch. ...after you eat lunch.
2. Do you brush your teeth before or after you get dressed?
3. What do we do before/after we go out for recess?
4. How did you know that the three pictures went together in a sequence?
5. How did you decide the order of the cards?
6. How do words help us tell about when something takes place? [Time order words such as early, later, before, and after help sequence events.]

Evidence of Learning
1. Check student work to make sure it shows a logical sequence.
2. Be sure student stories reflect the same sequence as the picture cards.

Extensions
1. Ask the children to find or draw pictures of events/actions and then describe what happened before and what happened after the event/action.
2. Have children draw a picture of something they do before school and something they do after school.
3. Make a sequence book of events or life cycles.
4. For a lot of laughter, have the students mix up the sequence of the pictures and tell the story.

* Reprinted with permission from *Principles and Standards for School Mathematics*, 2000 by the National Council of Teachers of Mathematics. All rights reserved.

Before and After

Line Up the Time

Topic
Ordering events

Key Question
What is the order of the events in our day?

Learning Goal
As a class, the students will sequence and illustrate the day's events.

Guiding Document
NCTM Standards 2000*
- *Recognize the attributes of length, volume, weight, area, and time*
- *Compare and order objects according to these attributes*
- *Develop common referents for measures to make comparisons and estimates*

Math
Measurement
   time

Integrated Processes
Observing
Comparing and contrasting
Classifying
Relating

Materials
For the class:
   string
   clothespins
   3- x 5-inch cards
   Before/After spinner
   one paper fastener

For each student:
   one *Event Cards* page
   one sentence strip

Management
1. Cut a length of string to serve as a clothesline. Give each child a clothespin.
2. Use *Event Cards* provided or unlined index cards to have the children create a set of pictures of events that happen during a day/week in the classroom.
3. Prior to the lesson, duplicate the *Before/After* spinner on card stock. Laminate for extended use.

Procedure
1. Gather the children as a whole group. Ask them to think about what happens during a day at school. Brainstorm a list of activities so that there will be a different activity for each student.
2. Have each child select an activity and illustrate it or choose an *Event Card* to represent it. Ask individuals to describe their pictures and then help them label their work.
3. Have one child bring up a picture and attach it to the line. Spin the *Before/After* spinner. Depending on where the spinner stops, invite someone who has a picture of an event that would come before (or after) that event to come forward and put the picture on the line. Repeat this process, having the children spin the spinner to determine if the picture added to the line will go before or after the previous picture, until all pictures have been hung on the line.

4. Follow up by having each child make a timeline crown with pictures of their day to wear home. Have them fold a sentence strip in half lengthwise, wrap it around their head and tape it. Allow the students to glue or tape event cards provided in this lesson to index cards or draw their own illustrations of events in their day on index cards. Tell the students to arrange the sequence of their day and slide the cards into their crowns in that order. Since the order can easily be changed, the students could rearrange the order of events based on each day's schedule and wear them more than one day.

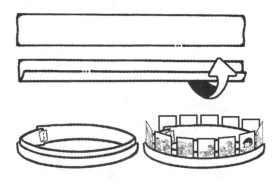

5. As children become familiar with each individual day's activities, start a picture timeline that could show events that occur during a week.

Discussion
1. What is the first thing we do every morning at school? ...the last thing?
2. What is something we do before lunch? ...after lunch?
3. What is something we do before library? ...after library?
4. Do we say the Pledge of Allegiance before or after calendar? What do we do after recess?
5. If you could arrange the class schedule for a day what would it look like? Explain your thinking.

Evidence of Learning
1. Watch as students place pictures on the clothesline. Check for accuracy in placing them in sequence.
2. Check individual student crowns for logical sequences of their days.

Extension
Graphing Opportunity: Ask each child to draw a picture of the first thing he or she does after arriving at school in the morning. Discuss pictures with the class and compare and contrast. Make a "First Thing in the Morning Graph." Do this over time and observe changes. Repeat this activity with the question "What is the last thing you do each night?"

* Reprinted with permission from *Principles and Standards for School Mathematics*, 2000 by the National Council of Teachers of Mathematics. All rights reserved.

Line Up the Time

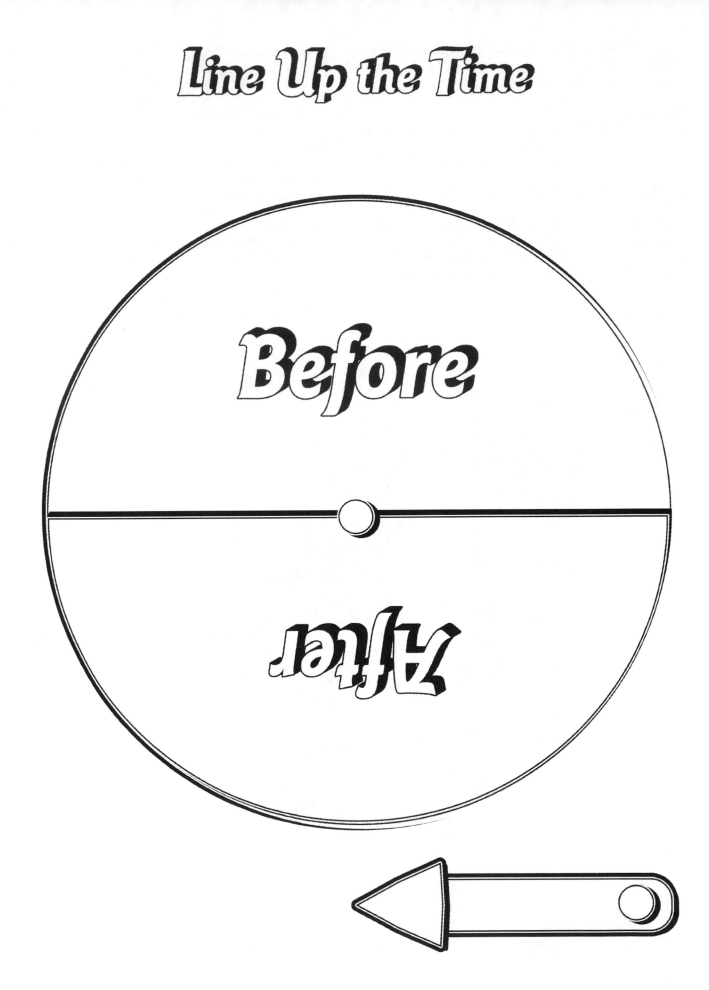

12

Quantifying Time

It is important for students to understand that the passage of time may be quantified through the use of customary and non-customary measures. Students need to understand that the attribute being measured is a time interval. The focus is for students to develop a sense of time intervals and to discover that different types of intervals exist. The experiences in this section address using interval measurements with a pendulum and a sand timer. Students will use the intervals as repeated units as well as a standard by which to evaluate the lengths of tasks.

Materials for this section:

- Metal washers, 2-inch
- Twist tie
- Masking tape
- Sand or salt
- Snow cone cups
- Unifix cubes
- Plastic bottles
- Hot glue gun and glue
- Drill and $\frac{3}{8}$" bit
- Plastic cups
- Pendulums
- Measuring cups

Time Counts

Topic
Quantifying time

Key Question
How can a pendulum help measure time?

Learning Goals
Students will:
1. use a pendulum to measure the passage of time, and
2. classify events based on the swings of a pendulum.

Guiding Document
NCTM Standards 2000
- *Recognize the attributes of length, volume, weight, area, and time*
- *Understand how to measure using nonstandard and standard units*
- *Use tools to measure*

Math
Measurement
    time
Estimation

Integrated Processes
Observing
Predicting
Comparing and contrasting

Materials
Metal washers, 2-inch (see *Management 1*)
Twist tie (see *Management 2*)
Masking tape
Time Counts recording page

Management
1. Students should work on this activity in pairs. You will need one washer for every two students.
2. Uncut twist tie can be purchased by the roll in the lawn and garden departments of most hardware stores. It can be cut easily using a good pair of scissors. Each pair of students will need one 18-inch length.

Procedure
1. Have students pair up. Distribute the washers and twist ties.

2. Direct the students to connect one end of the twist tie to a washer. Gather the class and demonstrate how to swing the pendulum. Tell the children to count each full cycle (a back and forth swing).
3. Show the students how to tape the twist tie to the side of a desk or table so that the washer can swing freely. Distribute masking tape and have each pair tape the pendulum to a desk.

4. Have the students swing their pendulums and count ten cycles. Repeat the swing/count activity and have the children stamp or clap each cycle.
5. Ask the children to predict whether or not they could sharpen a pencil before the pendulum completed ten cycles. Encourage them to test their predictions with a volunteer.
6. Challenge the students to find an activity that takes less than ten swings, one that takes more than ten swings and one that takes ten swings. Tell them to record their results on the *Time Counts* recording page.

Discussion
1. What were some of the activities that took longer than ten cycles?
2. What were some of the activities that you completed in less than ten cycles?
3. What activities took ten cycles?
4. If you repeated an activity, did it take the same number of cycles? Why or why not?

5. Did anyone else do the same activity? Did the number of cycles stay the same or was it different? Explain.
6. How did the pendulum help us measure time?

Evidence of Learning
1. Listen for the students to relate the number of swings to the length of time passed. For example, "Touching my nose doesn't take very long, I can do it in two swings of the pendulum."

Extensions
1. For further practice, prepare a set of picture cards depicting events such as sharpening a pencil, tying a shoe, etc. These cards could be digital pictures of your students performing certain tasks. Instruct partners to take turns drawing a card and completing the activity while the other partner uses the pendulum to determine the length of time it takes.
2. Allow the students to investigate with different lengths of pendulums. Have them time each pendulum for one minute and compare the number of cycles counted in one minute to the length of the pendulum.

* Reprinted with permission from *Principles and Standards for School Mathematics*, 2000 by the National Council of Teachers of Mathematics. All rights reserved.

Time Counts —Recording Sheet

More than 10 swings

10 swings

Less than 10 swings

Time in a Bottle!

Topic
Quantifying time

Key Question
How can sand help keep track of time?

Learning Goals
Students will:
1. describe how a sand timer works, and
2. use a sand timer to time classroom tasks.

Guiding Document
NCTM Standards 2000*
- *Recognize the attributes of length, volume, weight, area, and time*
- *Understand how to measure using nonstandard and standard units*
- *Use tools to measure*

Math
Measurement
    time
Estimation

Integrated Processes
Observing
Comparing and contrasting
Predicting
Identifying and controlling variables
Drawing conclusions

Materials
For the class:
    sand (or salt)
    snow cone cups (see *Management 2*)
    Unifix cubes
    measuring cups
    two plastic bottles, same size (see
      Management 4)
    hot glue gun and glue
    drill and bit
    plastic cups, 5 oz.
    pendulums (see *Management 3*)

For each student:
    Cone Cup page

Management
1. Bring in a sand table or sand tub.
2. Prior to the lesson, cut the ends off several snow cone cups so that there is a variety of opening sizes. Provide three cones with different size openings for each group. Label these cone *A*, *B,* and *C*.
3. Provide a tub of Unifix cubes and the pendulums used in *Time Counts.*
4. Prior to the activity, construct a simple sand timer made with two bottles and some salt or sand. To do this, use two plastic bottles of the same size (8-16 ounces) with lids. Remove the lids and with a glue gun, glue the two flat sides of the lids together. This procedure allows the bottles to be attached to the lids, with one bottle upright and the other inverted. In order to have sand or salt flow from one bottle to another, you will need to make an opening in the glued lids. With a small drill bit, approximately three-eighths inch, make a hole through both lids at the same time. Add enough sand so that it will take approximately one minute to pass through the opening you've drilled.

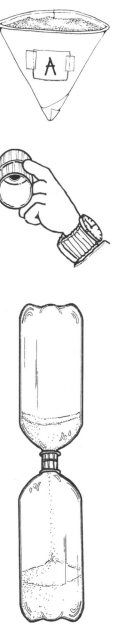

Procedure
Part One
1. Allow the children to explore using a cup of sand and snow cone cups with different-sized openings. Discuss whether or not they think the sand will run through the cones in the same amount of time. Tell the students to cover the holes in the bottom with their fingers and fill each cone with one cup of sand. Instruct the students to remove their fingers at the same time and observe the order in which the cups empty. Discuss the length of time that

the sand takes to go through the different-sized openings in terms of long time/short time.

2. Tell the students to refill cone *A* with a cup of sand as they did before. Using the pendulums from *Time Counts*, have students count the number of swings it takes for the cone to empty. Have the students record the size of the opening of the cone on the *Cone Cup* recording page by placing their pencil inside the upright snow cone and tracing the opening. Ask them to record the number of swings on the same page. Repeat this process with cones *B* and *C*. Discuss the length of time that the sand takes to go through the different-sized openings in terms of pendulum swings.

3. Repeat the process and instead of using the swings of the pendulum, have one student in each group snap together as many Unifix cubes as possible while their group tests each cone cup. Ask students to record their findings on the *Cone Cup* page. Compare the towers of Unifix cubes. Discuss the relationship between the size of the hole and the passage of time.

Part Two

1. After the exploration period, show the students a sand timer. Invert the timer and have the students watch the sand flow. Tell the students that you want them to predict whether they will be able to snap ten Unfix cubes together before the sand runs through. Invert the timer and have the children begin snapping the cubes.

2. Repeat the activity and compare the results of both tests.

3. Have the children brainstorm a list of activities that can be done in the classroom. From the list, select an activity and ask the children to predict whether it can be done before the sand runs through. Have a volunteer or partners do the activity and find out what happens.

Discussion

1. What did you notice about how fast the sand ran out of the cone cups? [The bigger the hole, the faster the sand went through.]

2. What were some of the activities that took longer than the flow of sand in the sand timer?

3. What were some of the activities that you completed before the sand finished?

4. If you repeated an activity, were the results the same? Explain.

5. Did anyone else do the same activity? Were the results the same or different? Explain.

6. If you use more sand, how will this change your results?

Evidence of Learning

1. Check the *Cone Cup* recording sheet. Look for accuracy in recording findings.

2. Watch as the students use the sand timer to time classroom tasks. Check to see that they are allowing the sand to completely empty before turning the timer over, etc.

* Reprinted with permission from *Principles and Standards for School Mathematics,* 2000 by the National Council of Teachers of Mathematics. All rights reserved.

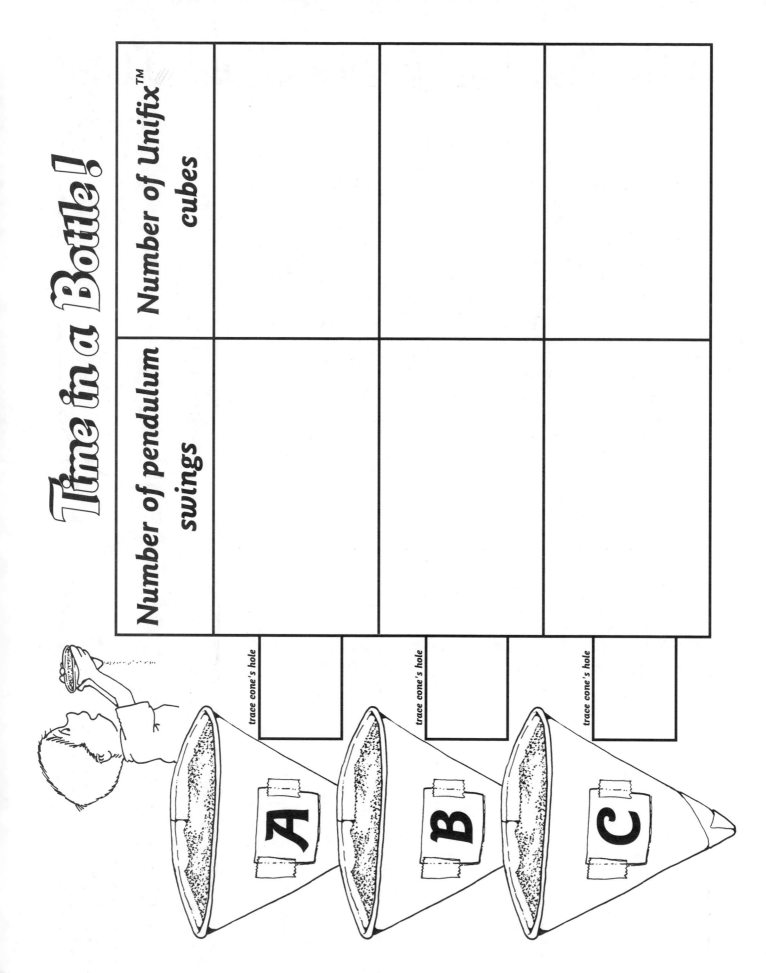

Time in a Bottle!

Number of pendulum swings	Number of Unifix™ cubes

trace cone's hole

trace cone's hole

trace cone's hole

A

B

C

Applications for the Sand Timer

The sand timer is a tool that measures the passage of time in informal units. It can be calibrated to measure a specific amount of time by varying the amount of sand used or the size of the opening the sand passes through. In these activities, the sand timer is used for two purposes: first, as a tool to look at the passage of time as short versus long; and secondly, as a calibrated timer used to time events.

Suggested uses measuring short vs. long periods of time:
Vary the sizes of timers and amounts of sand or salt in each timer for a comparison.
- Can you connect ten Unifix cubes before the sand runs out in each timer?
- Can you touch your toes ten times before the sand runs out in each timer?
- Create a short time/long time book. In it list things that take a short time to do and things that take a long time to do as determined by the sand timer.
- Which timer takes a short time to run out? ...a long time?

Suggested uses for the calibrated timer:
- Use the timer to know when the time at a center ends.
- See how many times you can write your name in one minute. ...in three minutes.
- Compare the analog clock in your classroom to your one-minute sand timer.
- Create a one-minute book. In it list things you can do in a minute. Use the sand timer to keep track of the minute.

Developing an Awareness of Clocks

Since timepieces are part of their daily lives, students need opportunities to look at a wide variety of them. They need to discover that there are many types and designs of clocks and watches. Some have Arabic numerals, some have Roman numerals, others have no numerals at all. The common thread that students need to understand is that all analog timepieces have position in common. A visual memory of the positions held by the numbers on the face of a clock needs to be developed and understood. For example, the 12 is always directly opposite of the six, and it is always at the top of the timepiece's face. Students need to develop this visual memory about position regardless of the design of the face of the timepiece. They also need to understand that the same time displayed using hands on an analog clock can be displayed without hands in a digital notation. The two activities that follow allow students to compare and contrast a variety of timepieces and help them to create that visual memory of analog timepieces by relating them to a number line.

Materials for this section:

- Pictures of analog and digital clocks and watches

Clocks, Clocks, and More Clocks

Topic
Awareness of clocks

Key Question
What do watches and clocks have in common?

Learning Goals
Students will:
1. examine a variety of clocks and watches,
2. sort clocks and watches, and
3. discuss how clocks and watches are similar and different.

Guiding Document
NCTM Standard 2000*
• *Recognize the attributes of length, volume, weight, area, and time*

Math
Measurement
   time

Integrated Processes
Observing
Comparing and contrasting
Classifying

Materials
Pictures of analog and digital clocks and watches (see *Management 1*)

Management
1. Collect an assortment of pictures of clocks or watches from magazines, catalogs, etc., or have students bring pictures in.
2. Prior to doing *Part One* of this activity, have a *no time day* in your classroom. On a *no time day* there shouldn't be any timekeeping devices visible and no regard should be given to time schedules. This means that your class will be unaware of recess time, lunchtime, etc. Cover any clocks in the room before you begin this *no time day*.

Procedure
Part One
1. Discuss any problems that may have occurred during your *no time day*. [missed recess, took too much time for reading and missed math, etc.]
2. Discuss the importance of timekeeping devices. Have the children close their eyes and visualize a

clock or a watch. Ask them to tell you where this watch or clock is located. Next, have them draw a picture of what they think a clock or a watch looks like. Then have the children share their drawings and compare and contrast the pictures with a partner or table group.
3. Have the students take a clock walk in search of timekeeping devices to see how many different clocks can be spotted in the school. Make note of the different sounds heard from each timepiece.

Part Two
1. Distribute the pictures of the clocks to the students. Have the children sort and compare the pictures of clocks and watches in as many ways as they are able. Discuss the sorting rules they use. Discuss the difference between Roman numerals and Arabic numerals.
2. To familiarize students with different types of timepieces, play *show me*. To do this, ask each child to select a picture of a watch or clock and to hold up their clock or watch if it has a particular characteristic such as Roman numerals. Have the students lower their timepiece pictures and repeat the process identifying other characteristics such as: Arabic numerals, no numerals, hands, no hands, etc. Discuss the fact that the timepieces may look different yet they serve the same purpose, to measure time.
3. Ask the children to brainstorm a list of ways that we use clocks and watches in our everyday life. Use an easel or a chalkboard for recording the list. Discuss what timepieces might be appropriate in specific situations. For example we would use a stopwatch to time a race, an alarm clock to wake us up, a watch or clock with a second hand to time seconds or minutes, etc.

Discussion
1. Where have you seen clocks?
2. What are some of the things that are the same on the clocks and watches? [numbers, hands, etc.]
3. What are some of the things that are found on some clocks and

watches but not on others? [brand names, second hand, Roman numerals, Arabic numbers, etc.]

4. List several different ways that we use clocks and watches?

5. What are some sounds that clocks and watches make?

Evidence of Learning

1. Look for accuracy in the grouping schemes the students use.

2. Listen for student explanations from the *Discussion* questions on how clocks and watches are alike and different.

Extensions

1. Ask the children to look for a clock at their house and make a drawing of it.

2. Direct the children to record the number of clocks at their houses and to record their findings on a class chart.

3. Ask the children to determine how many different types of clocks they have in their homes.

* Reprinted with permission from *Principles and Standards for School Mathematics*, 2000 by the National Council of Teachers of Mathematics. All rights reserved.

Clocks, Clocks, and More Clocks

Reading an Analog Clock

Learning to read an analog clock follows a developmental sequence. The first step is to be able to read a clock to the nearest hour. Students at this phase need to use just the hour hand of the clock. They need to develop an understanding that this hand moves at a different rate than the minute hand. The next developmental stage is to be able to read a clock to the nearest half and quarter hour. It is at this time the purpose of the minute hand is introduced to the students. Students are finally taught to read a clock to the nearest five-minute and one-minute intervals. The activities included in this section take the students through this developmental sequence using student-made clocks and model clocks.

Materials for this section:

- Sticky notes
- 12 sheets of $8\frac{1}{2}$" x 11" card stock
- Red card stock hour hand
- Blue card stock minute hand
- 12-inch ruler
- Yardstick or meter stick
- Red and blue masking tape
- Red and blue permanent markers
- Paper plates
- Small and large bobby pins
- Saturday morning cartoon schedule
- Sentence strips
- Pocket chart
- 48 blue circles
- Blue beanbag
- Big Time Learning Clock®

Hour by Hour

Topic
Awareness of the clock as a number line

Key Questions
How are the numbers on a clock similar to those on a number line?
How do we read an analog clock to nearest hour?

Learning Goals
Students will:
1. relate the numbers on a clock to those on a number line, and
2. read an analog clock to the nearest hour.

Guiding Document
*NCTM Standards 2000**
* *Recognize the attributes of length, volume, weight, area, and time*
* *Understand how to measure using nonstandard and standard units*

Math
Measurement
    time

Integrated Processes
Observing
Relating
Applying

Materials
Demonstration clock (see *Management 1*)
12 sheets of 8 $\frac{1}{2}$" x 11" card stock (see *Management 2*)
Red card stock hour hand (see *Management 3*)
12-inch ruler
Sticky notes
Red masking tape

Management
1. Construct a demonstration clock with numbers one to 12 in red. This can be done by using red magnetic numbers on a metal pizza pan or by writing the numbers one to 12 using a red permanent marker on a heavy-duty paper plate. The short red hour hand can be made by covering a piece of magnet strip with red masking tape for the magnetic clock or by covering a small bobby pin with red masking tape for the paper plate clock. To help the students develop a visual memory of the clock numbers, you need to be able to cover or remove the numbers on the demonstration clock.
2. On 12 sheets of 8 $\frac{1}{2}$" x 11" card stock, write the numbers one to 12 using a red marker.
3. Copy the hour hand on red card stock, cut it out and attach it to the end of the ruler to make an hour hand.

Procedure
1. Give each of 12 children one of the number cards and have them order themselves in a straight line from one to 12. Instruct the children to place their number under their arm and join hands with a classmate on each side. Emphasize how their line is like a number line. Invite the two end students to join hands and form a circle. Direct the students to turn to face the inside of the circle so that their number cards can be read from the center of the circle. Discuss how the number line has become a number "circle." Point out that if they go around the circle, the numbers increase until 12 and then start at one again.
2. Discuss how their number circle looks like a clock. Hold up the demonstration clock for the students to see the similarities. Explain that each number on the clock represents a time of day such as one o'clock, two o'clock, etc.
3. Place the hour hand in the center of the circle of children and ask the class, "What hour does the hand point to?" Repeat this process many times. Then point to a spot between two numbers and ask, "What number is it after?"
4. To help students develop a visual memory of the clock numbers, have the children in the 12, 3, 6, and 9 positions turn their number cards around so the numbers do not show. Point the hour hand to one of the "turned around" hours and ask, "What hour does the hand point to?" Point to a spot between two numbers and ask, "What number is it after?"
5. With the 12, 3, 6 and 9 cards turned to once again show the numbers, have children at 1, 2, 4, 5, 7, 8, 10, and 11 positions turn their cards around to hide their numbers. Point the hour hand to one of the "turned around" hours and ask the children, "To what hour does the hand point?" Point to a spot between two numbers and ask, "What hour is it after?"
6. Continue reinforcing the children's visual memories by using the demonstration clock. Cover the 12, 3, 6, and 9 using sticky notes and ask the students to

identify the covered numbers. Point the hour hand to the covered numbers and ask to what hour the hand is pointing.

7. Take the sticky notes off these numbers and cover the 1, 2, 4, 5, 7, 8, 10, and 11. Continue with the sequence described above.

Discussion

1. How is a clock like a number line?
2. What does the little hand on a clock tell us?
3. What hour falls between 12 and two on the clock?
4. What hour is after the four on a clock?
5. How did you know what the turned around numbers were?
6. What counting pattern is used on a clock?

Evidence of Learning

Listen for accuracy as children read the hour hands on a student clock.

* Reprinted with permission from *Principles and Standards for School Mathematics*, 2000 by the National Council of Teachers of Mathematics. All rights reserved.

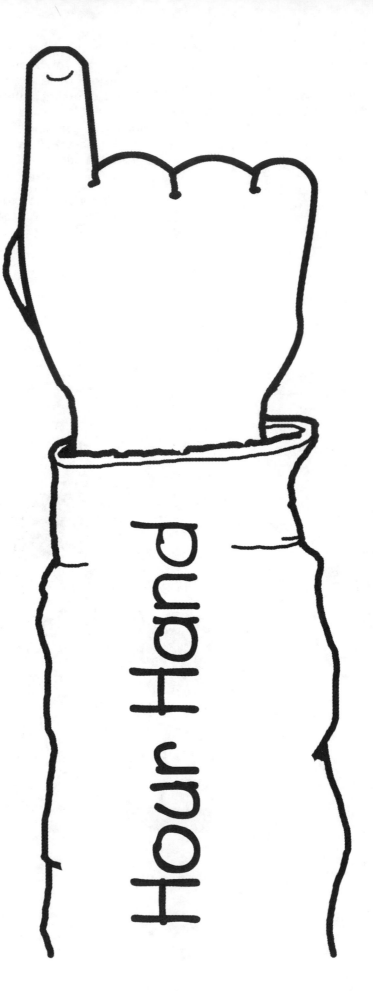

Hour Hand

Copy onto red card stock and attach to a 12-inch ruler.

Hands on the Hour

Topic
Reading an analog clock

Key Question
How can a model clock help us learn to tell time?

Learning Goals
Students will:
1. recognize relative positions of the hour numbers on the clock, and
2. use their model clocks to show where the hour hand would be positioned for times on the hour.

Guiding Document
NCTM Standards 2000*
* *Recognize the attributes of length, volume, weight, area, and time*
* *Understand how to measure using nonstandard and standard units*

Math
Measurement
    time

Integrated Processes
Observing
Relating
Applying

Materials
For the class:
    demonstration clock (see *Management 1*)
    sticky notes
    red tape
    red marking pens

For each student:
    paper plate
    small bobby pin

Management
1. Use the demonstration clock from *Hour by Hour.*
2. Prior to the lesson wrap one prong of each bobby pin with red tape for each student. The red tape will help connect the student model to commercial educational clock models.
3. Guide children through the construction of their own clocks with paper plates and bobby pins for hour hands.

Procedure
Part One—Teacher Demonstration
1. Position the hour hand of the class demonstration clock so that it points to a number from one to 12 and ask the class, "To what hour is the hand pointing?" Repeat this process several times. Then position the hour hand so that it points to a spot between two numbers and ask, "What number is the hour hand after?"
2. Cover the 12, 3, 6, and 9 on the demonstration clock with sticky notes. Point the hour hand to one of the "covered" hours and ask the children, "To what hour is the hour hand pointing?" Point to a spot between two numbers and ask, "What number is it after?"
3. Uncover the 12, 3, 6, and 9 on the demonstration clock and cover the 1, 2, 4, 5, 7, 8, 10 and 11 numbers. Point the hour hand to one of the "covered" hours and ask the children, "What hour is the hour hand pointing to?" Point to a spot between two numbers and ask, "What number is it after?"

Part Two—Student Clocks
1. Have each child use a paper plate to make a clock face using a red marker to write the numbers 1–12. Insert a small red bobby pin into the center of each plate to represent the hour hand.
2. To check for understanding, ask the children to *match, show,* and *tell* different hour settings on their clocks.
3. Set the demonstration clock hour hand to the number five. Ask students to *match* the demonstration clock by setting their clocks to the same time. If they can correctly *match* their clocks to the demonstration clock, proceed with the next step.
4. Have several students set their clocks for different times on the hour such as three o'clock, ten o'clock, and two o'clock. Ask other students to *show* the clock that is set for ten o'clock, three o'clock, etc., by pointing to the clocks that are set for the designated times.
5. Finally, have students set their clocks for different times on the hour and ask others to *tell* the set times shown on their classmates' clocks.

Discussion
1. On the clock face, what numbers come before and after 10? ...before and after one? etc.
2. If it is five o'clock, what time was it one hour earlier? What time will it be one hour later?
3. To which number would the hour hand point in order to show the time you go to bed?

Evidence of Learning
Look for accuracy as students match, show, and tell time to the hour.

IT'S ABOUT TIME!

Time by Fives

Topic
Reading an analog clock

Key Question
How does a counting pattern of five help us tell time?

Learning Goal
Students will identify minutes after the hour in five-minute intervals.

Guiding Document
NCTM Standards 2000*
- *Recognize the attributes of length, volume, weight, area, and time*
- *Understand how to measure using nonstandard and standard units*
- *Use tools to measure*

Math
Measurement
    time

Integrated Processes
Observing
Relating
Applying

Materials
Number cards on card stock (see *Management 1*)
Blue card stock minute hand (see *Management 2*)
Yardstick or meter stick
Blue beanbag
Blue marker

Management
1. Use a blue marker to write the multiples of five from five to 60 on 12 sheets of $8\frac{1}{2}$" x 11" card stock.
2. Tape a large blue card stock minute hand to the end of a yardstick or meter stick to make a minute hand.

Procedure
Part One
1. Invite 12 students to the front of the room. Ask each student to hold up one hand, showing all five fingers. Have the class assist you in counting the fingers by fives. [five, ten, 15, up to 60]
2. Distribute the number cards to 12 children and have them order themselves in a straight line from five to 60. Have the class once again assist you in counting by fives.
3. Have the children form a circle by having the child with the number 60 stand to the right of the child

with the number five. Place one child in the center of the circle holding a beanbag. Call out a multiple of five (e.g., 20) and have the child in the center toss the beanbag to identify the matching numbers. Tell the students in the 15, 30, and 45 positions to turn their number cards around and continue tossing the bag and identifying the numbers, including the numbers not showing.
4. Repeat this process to give multiple children the opportunity to be in the center.

Part Two
1. Distribute the number cards to 12 children and have them arrange themselves as they did in *Part One*. Hold up the demonstration clock so students can see the similarities. Discuss how the counting pattern of five helps us tell time. Explain that each number on these clocks represents a five-minute interval of time such as five, ten, 15 minutes, etc. Tell the students that there is a special big hand on the clock that always points to the number of minutes. Show the class the large minute hand.
2. Place the minute hand in the center of the circle. Point the minute hand to one of the numbers and ask the children, "How many minutes does the hand point to?"
3. Point to a spot between two numbers and ask, "What number of minutes is it before?" or "What number of minutes is it after?"
4. To develop a visual memory of the clock, have the children in the 15, 30, 45, and 60 minute positions turn the number cards around. Point the minute hand to one of the cards and ask the children, "How many minutes does the hand show?" Point to a spot between two numbers and ask, "What number is it before?" or "What number is it after?"
5. With the 60, 15, 30, and 45 cards facing out, have the children at the 5, 10, 20, 25, 35, 40, 50, and 55 minute positions turn their number cards around. Point the yardstick or meter stick to one of the cards that is turned around and ask, "How many minutes does the hand show?" Point to a spot

between two numbers and ask, "What number is it before?" or "What number is it after?"

Discussion

1. What does the big hand on a clock tell us? What does the little hand we studied earlier tell us?
2. If you are counting by fives, what number falls between 40 and 50?
3. If you are counting by fives, what number comes before 30 on a clock? ...after 30?
4. If the big hand is on the 25, how many minutes past the hour is it?
5. As we count by fives around the clock, what number of minutes is across from the 60 on a clock?
6. As we count by fives around the clock, what number of minutes is across from the 15 on a clock?

7. How are the hour numbers different than the minute numbers?

Evidence of Learning

Listen for accuracy as students read the clock in five-minute intervals.

Extension

After extended practice with this format, have a child stand in the center with one arm extended as the minute hand and repeat the procedure.

* Reprinted with permission from *Principles and Standards for School Mathematics*, 2000 by the National Council of Teachers of Mathematics. All rights reserved.

Minute Hand

Copy onto blue card stock
and attach to a yardstick.

Double Time

Topic
Reading an analog clock

Key Question
How can we use the minute hand of a clock to show five-minute intervals?

Learning Goal
Students will set a clock to show the time in five-minute intervals.

Guiding Document
NCTM Standards 2000*
- *Recognize the attributes of length, volume, weight, area, and time*
- *Understand how to measure using nonstandard and units*

Math
Measurement
 time

Integrated Processes
Observing
Relating
Applying

Materials
For the class:
 demonstration clock (see *Management 1*)
 sticky notes
 blue tape
 blue marker

For each student:
 paper plate
 large bobby pins

Management
1. Prepare a demonstration clock with the minutes numbered in blue and a blue minute hand. This can be done by using blue magnetic numbers on a metal pizza pan or by writing the multiples of five from five to 60 using a blue permanent marker on a heavy-duty paper plate. The blue minute hand can be made by covering a piece of magnetic strip with blue masking tape for the pizza pan clock or by covering a large bobby pin with blue masking tape for the paper plate clock. To help the students develop a visual memory of the clock numbers, you need to be able to cover or remove the numbers on the demonstration clock.

2. Guide the students through the construction of their paper plate clocks with multiples of five (5–60) written in blue.
3. To serve as a minute hand, wrap blue tape around one prong of a bobby pin for each student. This color will provide a bridge to the commercial clock the students will be using later.

Procedure
1. On the demonstration clock, point the minute hand to one of the numbers and ask the children, "How many minutes does the hand show?" Indicate a spot between two numbers and ask, "What number is it before?" or "What number is it after?"
2. Using sticky notes, cover the minute numbers of 60, 15, 30, and 45 on the demonstration clock. Point the minute hand to one of the "covered" numbers and ask the children, "How many minutes does the hand show?" Indicate a spot between two numbers and ask, "What number is it before?" or "What number is it after?"
3. Uncover the 60, 15, 30 and 45 on the demonstration clock, and using sticky notes, cover the minute numbers of 5, 10, 20, 35, 50, and 55. Point the minute hand to one of the "covered" numbers and ask the children, "How many minutes does the hand show?" Indicate a spot between two numbers and ask, "What number of minutes is it before?" or "What number of minutes is it after?"
4. Have each child use a paper plate to make a clock face. Insert a bobby pin in the center of each plate to be used as a minute hand.

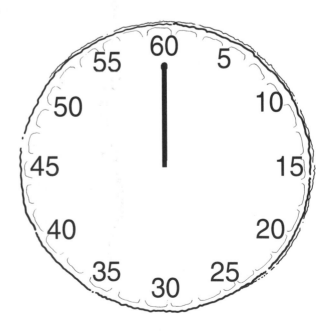

5. To check for understanding, ask the children to *match, show,* and *tell* different minute settings on their clocks.

6. Set the demonstration clock minute hand to the number 15. Ask students to *match* the demonstration clock by setting their clocks to the same time. If they can correctly *match* their clocks to the demonstration clock, proceed with the next step.

7. Have several students set their clocks for different times on the minute, such as 10, 55, and 30. Ask other students to *show* the clock that shows the minute hand pointing to 30 minutes, 55 minutes, etc. by pointing to the clocks that are set for the designated times.

8. Finally, have students set their clocks for different times on the minute and ask others to *tell* the set times shown on their classmates' clocks.

Discussion

1. How is a minute hand on a clock different than an hour hand?
2. How many minutes past the hour is it when the big hand is straight down?
3. What is the number pattern when you are counting minutes on these clocks? [count by fives]
4. How is counting by fives useful in telling time?

Evidence of Learning

Check for accuracy as students match, show, and tell time in five-minute intervals.

Name That Time

Topic
Reading an analog clock

Key Question
How do we use both hands of a clock to tell time?

Learning Goal
Using flip cards, students will role-play and read clocks with minute and hour hands.

Guiding Document
NCTM Standard 2000*
- *Recognize the attributes of length, volume, weight, area, and time*

Math
Measurement
    time

Integrated Processes
Observing
Relating
Applying

Materials
Number cards (see *Management 1*)
Minute and hour hands (see *Management 1*)

Management
1. Use the number cards 1-12 and 5-60 and the minute and hour hands previously used in *Hour by Hour* and *Time by Fives*.
2. Join the number cards together by stacking the one card on top of the five card, the two on top of the 10, the three on top of the 15, etc. Tape the card pairs together along the top edge.

3. Note to the teacher: When the hands on a clock rotate, they do so simultaneously. In this activity, children are representing clocks using their own bodies, without gears, and hour and minute hands made from paper. The hands will not move simultaneously. Since this is a beginning lesson in reading a clock with both hour and minute hands, and so that the students are not overwhelmed, it is suggested that the movement of the hour hand into positions after the hour numbers be discussed

at a later time. In this lesson, when setting the clocks, students will be asked to position the hour hands directly on the hour numbers. (See *How Time Flies* for instruction in the simultaneous movement of the hour and minute hands.)

Procedure
Part One
1. Distribute the number cards to 12 children and have them arrange themselves in a circle to represent a clock. Remind them of the placement of the 12 at the top, the six at the bottom, and the three and nine directly across from each other.
2. Introduce the word clockwise as you review the counting sequence of the hour numbers (1-12) and the counting sequence of the minutes using five-minute intervals (5-60). Discuss instances where they have used the word clockwise. [Play in a game usually rotates in a clockwise manner.]
3. Ask the students holding the clock numbers to turn the cards so that only the hour numbers (1-12) show. Point the hour hand to the nine and the minute hand to the 12. Explain that when the minute hand points to the 12, they are to use the name of the number to which the hour hand is pointing with a last name of *o'clock*. In this case, nine o'clock would be the appropriate response.
4. Leave the minute hand pointing to the number 12, and position the hour hand to point to the number five. Discuss how to read the clock: The first name is five and the last name is o'clock. [five o'clock]
5. Continue resetting the student circle clock having the students call out the time represented. It is suggested that at this point you ask students to only name on-the-hour times.
6. Be sure all students have the opportunity to be a part of the human clock.

Part Two

1. To introduce reading time on the half-hour, position the hands on the student circle clock to five o'clock. Direct the children to look at the clock hands and to determine the time. [five o'clock]

2. Leaving the hour hand pointed to the number five, direct the students to watch as you move the minute hand to point to the numeral six. As you move the minute hand over the numbers one through five, point out to the students that the minute hand is passing these numbers in order to get to the number six position. It is moving in a clockwise direction.

3. Discuss the numbers to which each hand is pointing. [The minute hand is pointing to the six and the hour hand is pointing to the five.] Explain that once the minute hand moves from the 12 position, the hour loses its o'clock last name. It takes on a new name according to the hidden number to which the minute hand is pointing.

4. Remind the students of the hidden numbers. Discuss how these numbers followed the counting pattern of 5, 10, 15, 20, 25, ...through 60.

5. Have them trace the path the minute hand traveled from the number 12 to the number six by pointing to the numbers one through six as they count by fives. Each time they get to the next number, have them lift the hour numbers to check their counting. When at the number one, they should see a five under the card and should say five. When at the number two, they should see a ten under the card and should be on the count of ten, etc. Once they reach the number six position, they should find the hidden number 30 under the card and should be at the count of 30. Explain that when the clock's hands are in this position, the time is read as five-thirty.

6. Ask the students to reset the student circle clock to show seven o'clock. Then have them move the minute hand to point to the six. Have the students count by fives, naming the hidden numbers as they move the minute hand from the 12 to the six position.

7. Have them read the time shown on the clock. [seven-thirty]

8. Continue with this sequence of experiences until the students seem comfortable reading their student circle clocks.

Discussion

1. What does it mean to have a hidden number on a clock?

2. If your arms and hands were the hands on a clock, what directions would they be pointing to show three o'clock?

3. What is special about the counting sequence of five and telling time on a clock?

4. What is time's last name when the minute hand is on the hidden number 60?

Evidence of Learning

Listen for accurate reading of the clock as students use both hands to read time on the student clock.

Extension

As an introductory lesson on elapsed time, have the students start at a specific time, like 2:00, and ask them what time it would be in two hours. Allow them to physically move the hour hand around the clock to the next time.

* Reprinted with permission from *Principles and Standards for School Mathematics,* 2000 by the National Council of Teachers of Mathematics. All rights reserved.

Two Timers

Topic
Reading an analog clock

Key Question
How do the two clock faces from the *Hidden Numbers Clock* combine to help us read an analog clock?

Learning Goal
Students will read analog clocks to the nearest hour and half-hour.

Guiding Document
NCTM Standard 2000*
- *Recognize the attributes of length, volume, weight, area, and time*

Math
Measurement
  time

Integrated Processes
Observing
Relating
Applying

Materials
For the class:
  Hidden Numbers demonstration clock
    (see *Management 1*)
  Saturday morning cartoon schedule
    (see *Management 3*)
  red and blue tape
  sentence strips
  pocket chart

For each student:
  2 paper plates
  one large and one small bobby pin

Management
1. Prepare a *Hidden Numbers* demonstration clock with both hour and minute numbers. (See *Directions for the Number Clock*.) Wrap one prong of each large bobby pin with blue tape, and one prong of each small bobby pin with red tape.
2. Prior to the lesson, have each student construct a *Hidden Numbers Clock* with paper plates and bobby pins.

3. You will need to have a copy of the Saturday morning cartoon schedule. The cartoon shows will need to be written on sentence strips and displayed in a pocket chart. Be sure to include the time each show begins.

4. Note to the teacher: When the hands on a clock rotate, they do so simultaneously. In this activity, children are using paper clocks without gears, therefore, the hands will not move simultaneously. Since this is a beginning lesson in reading a clock with both minute and hour hands, and so that the students are not overwhelmed, it is suggested that the movement of the hour hand into positions after the hour numbers be addressed at a later time. In this lesson, when setting the clocks to the half-hour, students are asked to position the hour hands directly on the hour numbers. (See *How Time Flies* for instruction in the simultaneous movement of the hour and minute hands.)

Procedure
Part One
1. Position the demonstration clock hands to three o'clock. Have children look at the clock's hands.
2. Discuss the number to which the minute hand is pointing [12] and the number to which the hour

hand is pointing [3]. Review the fact that when the minute hand points to the 12, the name of the number to which the hour hand is pointing has a last name of *o'clock*. In this case, three o'clock would be the appropriate response. Have students set their paper clocks to match the demonstration clock.

3. Using their *Hidden Numbers Clocks*, ask the students to leave the minute hands pointing to the number 12 and to position the hour hands to point to the number five. Discuss how to read the clocks. [The first name is five and the last name is o'clock—five o'clock] Reset the demonstration clock to help those students who are struggling. Have them match their paper clocks to the demonstration clock showing five o'clock.

4. Continue having the students reset their clocks, reading the time to the hour.

5. To check for understanding, have the students match, show, and tell designated times using their *Hidden Numbers Clocks*. First, set the demonstration clock to a specific time to the hour. Ask students to match the demonstration clock by setting their clocks to the same time.

6. Have several students set their clocks for different times on the hour such as three o'clock, five o'clock, and two o'clock. Ask other students to show the clock that is set for five o'clock, three o'clock, etc.

7. Finally, have students set their clocks for different times on the hour and ask others to tell the set times shown on their classmates' clocks.

8. Continue with this type of exercise until students are able to name the time on the hour.

9. Assign on-the-hour times that occur during the school day to students in your class. Set an alarm clock to chime at those hours during the day. When the alarm sounds, have the student that was assigned that particular time stand up, show his or her paper clock, and say, "It's ___ o'clock and I'm here to say, 'When the hands of the clock look this way, I'll stand up tall to proudly chime, the number of counts will tell the time.'" (The students should "chime" one time for each hour.) Have all students reset their paper clocks to match the alarm clock. Discuss how to read the time shown on the alarm clock and on their matching paper clocks.

Part Two
1. Position the demonstration clock hands to three o'clock. Ask the children to determine the time and set their paper clocks to match the demonstration clock.

2. Invite the students to watch as you move the minute hand on the demonstration clock to point to the number six, leaving the hour hand pointed

to the number three. Point out the numbers one through five that the minute hand is passing before getting to the number six position. Direct the students to do the same on the paper clocks.

3. Discuss the numbers to which each hand is pointing. [The minute hand is pointing to the six, and the hour hand is pointing to the three.] Explain that once the minute hand moves from the 12 position, the hour loses its "o'clock" last name. It takes on a new name according to the hidden number to which the minute hand is pointing.

4. Remind the students of the hidden numbers they counted while in their student circle clock. Discuss how these numbers followed the counting pattern of five, 10, 15, 20, 25, ...through 60.

5. Have them trace the clockwise path the minute hand traveled from the number 12 to the number six by pointing to the numbers one through six as they count by fives. Each time they get to the next number, have them lift the tabs to check their counting. When at the number one, they should see a five under the tab and should say five. When at the number two, they should see a ten under the tab and should be on the count of ten, etc. Once they reach the number six position, they should find the hidden number 30 under the tab and should be at the count of 30.

6. Have the students lift the number six tabs on their clocks to find the hidden number 30. Explain that when the clock's hands are in this position, the time is read as three-thirty.

7. Ask the students to reset their clocks to show five o'clock. Then have them move the minute hand to point to the six. Have the students count by fives, naming the hidden numbers as they move the minute hand from the 12 to the six position.

8. Have them read the time shown on their clocks. [five-thirty] Reset the demonstration clock to help those students who are struggling. Invite them to match their paper clocks to the demonstration clock.

9. Continue having the students reset their clocks, reading the time to the hour and half-hour for several days.

10. To check for understanding, have the students match, show, and tell designated times using their *Hidden Numbers Clocks*. First, set the demonstration clock to a specific time to the half-hour. Ask students to match the demonstration clock by setting their clocks to the same time.

11. Have several students set their clocks for different times on the half-hour such as three-thirty, five-thirty, and two-thirty. Ask other students to show the clock that is set for five-thirty, three-thirty, etc.

12. Finally, have students set their clocks for different times on the half-hour and ask others to tell the set times shown on their classmate's clocks.

13. Continue with this type of exercise until students demonstrate an ability to name the times on the paper clocks.

14. At various times throughout the day, set an alarm clock to ring on the half-hour. When the alarm sounds, have the students reset their paper clocks to match the alarm clock. Discuss how to read the time showing on the alarm clock and on their matching paper clocks.

Part Three
1. Direct the students' attention to the pocket chart that contains the Saturday morning cartoon schedule.

2. Select a cartoon show. Ask the students to use their clocks to display the time the program begins. Repeat with several shows that require the students to display the times to the hour and half-hour.

3. Ask the students to position the hands of their clocks to show the time their favorite cartoons come on.

4. Direct the students to sequence the times they have displayed on their clocks by having them come to the front of the room one at a time. Have each student come and place his or her clock in the correct position relative to the time on the first student clock. Each student will need to state the time his or her clock shows and if it comes before, after, or at same time as the first clock.

5. Group the students by the times they have chosen. For example: all the students that have 8:00 would be in one group, all the students with 8:30 would be in another group, etc.

Discussion
1. Show the hour (minute) hand.
2. If it is 9:30, show where the hour hand and the minute hand would be.
3. What time is it if the minute hand is on the six and the hour hand is on the 12?
4. Describe the hour hand. ...the minute hand.
5. Where will the hands be when it is one o'clock?
6. How does telling time to the nearest hour and half-hour help you with your TV viewing schedule?
7. When the large hand is pointing to the six, how many minutes past the hour does it show?

Evidence of Learning
Check individual student clocks for accuracy in setting the specific times.

* Reprinted with permission from *Principles and Standards for School Mathematics*, 2000 by the National Council of Teachers of Mathematics. All rights reserved.

Two Timers

Directions for the Hidden Number Clock

Materials
Two thin paper plates
Bobby pins, one large and one small
Scissors
Blue and red markers

Procedure

1. Fold one thin paper plate into fourths.
2. With the fold lines as a guide, use a blue marker to write the anchor numbers 60, 15, 30, and 45 on the first paper plate. When you are comfortable with the spacing, add the additional numbers 5, 10, 20, 25, 35, 40, 50, and 55 between the anchor numbers. Place this plate of hidden numbers to the side while constructing the clock face.
3. Fold a second plate into fourths.
4. With the fold lines as a guide, use a red marker to write the anchor numbers 12, 3, 6, and 9, on the second paper plate, as they appear on a clock. (These numbers should fit directly over the hidden numbers 60, 15, 30, and 45 when the two plates are connected.)
5. Attach the two plates together by placing a small hole in the center of the plates and inserting the bobby pins. The bottom plate should have the hidden numbers 5, 10, 15, etc., and the top plate should have the numbers 1, 2, 3, etc.
6. When you are comfortable with the alignment of the two plates, use a red marker to add the additional numbers 1, 2, 4, 5, 7, 8, 10, and 11 between the anchor numbers. (These numbers should be directly over the hidden numbers 5, 10, 20, 25, 35, 40, 50, and 55.)
7. Separate the two plates by placing your fingers between them. Cut tabs into the rim of the top plate by cutting slits on both sides of each of the numbers. When these tabs are folded back, the hidden numbers should be revealed.

Minute by Minute

Topic
Reading an analog clock

Key Question
How do you read a clock to the nearest minute?

Learning Goal
Students will construct and read a student clock to the nearest minute.

Guiding Document
NCTM Standard 2000*
- *Recognize the attributes of length, volume, weight, area, and time*

Math
Measurement
   time

Integrated Processes
Observing
Relating
Applying

Materials
Number cards (see *Management 1*)
Minute and hour hands (see *Management 1*)
Blue circles (see *Management 2*)

Management
1. Use the number cards 1-12 that flip to show the multiples of five from 5-60, and the minute and hour hands previously used in *Two Timers*.
2. Cut 48 blue paper circles (seven inches in diameter) to represent minute intervals. These will be placed between the numbers in the student circle clock. On one side of the dots write the numbers, 1-59 excluding the multiples of five.
3. Note to the teacher: When the hands on a clock rotate, they do so simultaneously. In this activity, the hands of the clocks the students are using will not move simultaneously. Since this is a beginning lesson in reading a clock with hour and minute hands, and so the students are not overwhelmed, it is suggested that the movement of the hour hand into positions after the hour numbers be discussed through a later lesson. In this lesson, when setting the clocks, students will be asked to position the hour hands directly on the hour numbers. (See *How Time Flies* for instruction in the simultaneous movement of the hour and minute hands.)

Procedure
1. Distribute the number cards to 12 children and have them arrange themselves in a circle to represent a clock. Remind them of the placement of the 12 at the top, the six at the bottom, and the three and nine directly across from each other.
2. Review the counting sequence of the hour numbers one to 12 and the counting sequence of the minutes using five-minute intervals from five to 60.
3. Discuss how the students have counted by fives, but that sometimes it is necessary to count the numbers in between. Have the students holding the hour numbers flip their cards so that only the minute numbers are showing.
4. Ask the children to help place blue circles, number side down, between each number to show the minutes between the fives. Starting with the number 60, have them place four circles before the five-minute number. Continue placing four circles between each two numbers.
5. Using the minute hand, ask the students to count aloud while pointing to each circle and minute number. [one, two, three, four, **five**, six, ...**60**] Discuss how the multiples of five are also representing a minute just as the circles do, but that the numbers help us to remember our count.
6. Point the minute hand to any circle on the clock. Help the students count-on to determine the minute indicated. Turn the circle over to verify the answer. Continue to give the students practice naming the minutes.
7. Once the students demonstrate an understanding of the minutes, add the hour hand to the student circle clock.
8. Ask the students holding the clock numbers to flip the cards so that only the hour numbers one to 12 show. Point the hour hand to eight and the minute hand to the four. Ask the students to name the time represented on the clock. Students may respond eight-four. Remind them that the minute hand points to the hidden numbers. Give them another chance to respond with eight-twenty. Turn the number card over to reveal the 20.
9. Discuss what this time means. Ask them to count the circles and numbers from the top of the clock, starting just after the 12 and ending at the number four on the clock. As the students count, slowly

move the minute hand across each corresponding circle and number. Explain that this clock indicates that 20 minutes have passed since it was eight o'clock, and that the time can be read as eight-twenty.
10. Continue with this sequence of experiences until the students seem comfortable reading their student circle clock.

Discussion
1. Point to and describe the hour hand. ...the minute hand.
2. If it were 9:30, where would the hour hand and the minute hand be? [The hour hand would be on the 9 and the minute hand would be on the 6.]
3. If the minute hand is three blue circles past the six and the hour hand is on the 12, what time is it? [12:33]
4. Where will the hands be when it is one o'clock? [on the one and the 12]

5. What hidden numbers does the minute hand pass when traveling from the 12 position to the six position on the clock? [one-thirty]
6. Which numbers on the clock tell the hour? [one through 12]
7. Which numbers on the clock does the minute hand point to? [one through 60]
8. What happens on a clock when it goes from the fifty-ninth minute to the sixtieth minute?
9. Why does a clock have two hands?

Evidence of Learning
Listen for accuracy as students read the student clock to the nearest minute.

*   Reprinted with permission from *Principles and Standards for School Mathematics*, 2000 by the National Council of Teachers of Mathematics. All rights reserved.

How Time Flies

Topic
Reading an analog clock

Key Question
How do you read an analog clock to the nearest minute?

Learning Goals
Students will:
1. explore the connection between the movement of the minute hand and the hour hand, and
2. identify minute intervals on a clock.

Guiding Document
NCTM Standard 2000*
- *Recognize the attributes of length, volume, weight, area, and time*

Math
Measurement
    time

Integrated Processes
Observing
Applying
Relating

Materials
Big Time Learning Clocks®
How Time Flies student book

Management
1. Big Time Learning Clocks® are available through the AIMS catalog. If other clocks are available to you, make sure that their hour and minute hands move simultaneously. You will need one clock for each student.
2. Duplicate several copies of the *How Time Flies* page of the student book for each child.
3. Note to the teacher: A student who demonstrates the ability to read all the possible time positions on these clocks is only demonstrating an understanding of how to "read" a clock. This does not indicate an understanding of time. Additional experiences are needed to help the young learner construct an understanding of a minute, an hour, passage of time, elapsed time, etc.

Procedure
Part One
1. Give each student a Big Time Learning Clock®. Ask the students to look at their clocks and to discuss what they notice about them.

2. Discuss how the minute hands are blue and longer than the red hour hands. Talk about how the minute numbers are blue to match the minute hands, and how the red hour numbers match the red hour hands. Tell the students that they will watch the minute hand move around the clock as time "flies by."
3. Point out the small blue circles and have the students count the circles beginning at the first circle after the number 60 and ending at the red number one. [1, 2, 3, 4, 5] Have them continue counting the circles after the blue number five, stopping at the blue number 10.
4. Continue this counting around the clock until they reach the number 12 and the minute number 60. Ask the students to point to a blue circle between the minute numbers five and ten. Have them count-on, beginning with five, until they reach the chosen blue circle, and to name the counting number. [6, 7, 8, or 9] Many times over several days have the students choose a circle, count, and name the minutes.
5. To check for understanding, have the students match, show, and tell the minute numbers. Set the minute hand to read 16 and ask students to match this clock by setting their clocks to read the same. Once the students can match clocks, set several different clocks with different minute hand settings. Ask the students to show a clock where the minute hand points to 22, 46, 55, etc. When students demonstrate an understanding of this task, continue by setting several clocks with different minute hand positions. Point to a clock and ask the students to tell the position of the minute hand.

Part Two
1. Give each student a Big Time Learning Clock®. Ask the students to try to set their clocks to show eight o'clock by gently moving the red hour hand to eight. Discuss how this is not possible with these clocks.
2. Tell them to try moving the blue minute hand clockwise, around and around the clock face and to observe what happens to the red hour hand. Discuss that as the blue minute hand moves around the clock, the red hour hand begins to move as well. Discuss how the red hour hand will not move unless the blue minute hand moves.
3. Ask the students to move their blue minute hands clockwise, around and around until the red hour hands are pointing to the number eight. Tell the students to count the blue dots and blue numbers as they slowly move the blue minute hands one

time around the clock. Ask them to tell where the red hour hands are now. Have the students read the time showing on their clocks. [nine o'clock]

4. Continue having the students move the minute hands completely around the clocks, pointing out the changes in the positions of the hour hands. Have them count from one to 60 as the minute hand travels around the clock.

5. Tell the students that they can take a short cut in their counting by counting by fives while moving the minute hands around the clocks. After each hour, have the students name the times shown on the clocks.

6. Continue having the students move the minute hands around the clocks, counting, and noting the time on the hour. Once the students begin to demonstrate an understanding of this movement, stop the minute hand at different intervals, and have the students describe the position of the red hour hands. Point out how the hour hand is halfway between the last hour and the next hour when the minute hand is pointing to the six position, or the minute number 30.

7. Give the students many experiences moving the minute hands around while noting the positions of the hour hands.

8. To help the students understand how to name the times shown on their clocks, have them say the time for each blue circle and number position. For example, have them set the beginning time to nine o'clock. While slowly moving the blue minute hand, have the students say, nine o-one, nine o-two, nine o-three, nine o-four, nine o-five, ... to nine-ten.

9. Have the students observe that when the hour hand points to a number, it is on the hour—two o'clock or three o'clock. When the hour hand has moved away from the number, the time is past that hour.

Part Three
1. Give students the book cover and several copies of the *How Time Flies* page. Have them staple these copies together to construct a time book.
2. Ask the students to draw the hands on the clocks to represent a time of day or night.
3. Ask them to write about an event that may take place at this time.

Discussion
1. Identify the hour hand. ...the minute hand.
2. Describe the hour hand. ...the minute hand. [The hour hand is small and red; the minute hand is large and blue.]
3. Why do you think the hour hand and minute hand on a clock have different lengths?
4. If it is 9:32, show where the hour hand and the minute hand would be.
5. It is five minutes after one o'clock. Where should the hands on the clock be?
6. If the minute hand is on the three and the hour hand is near the 12, what time is it? [12:15]
7. Where will the hands be when it is 1:10? [The hour hand will be slightly to the right of the one and the minute hand will be on the 2.]
8. What counting patterns can be found on a clock? [1-12 and multiples of five from 5-60]

Evidence of Learning
1. Listen for questions and comments that show an understanding of the connection between the movement of the minute hand and the hour hand.
2. Listen for accuracy as students identify minute intervals on a clock.

* Reprinted with permission from *Principles and Standards for School Mathematics*, 2000 by the National Council of Teachers of Mathematics. All rights reserved.

How Time Flies

It is_____o'clock

It is time to_____

Reading a Digital Clock

Students need to understand and develop a visual memory for the position of the numbers on the face of a digital clock just as they do for an analog clock. Regardless of the shape, size, or decorative face of the digital clock, the numbers to the left of the colon represent the hours and the numbers to the right of the colon represent the minutes. Students often have less difficulty learning to read a digital clock than an analog clock. However, they need to understand the relationship between the analog clock and a digital clock. The activities in this section address the similarities and differences between the two types of clocks.

Materials for this section:

- Cylindrical containers
- Overhead markers, red and blue
- Utility knife
- Binder rings, 10
- Dowels, 5
- Card stock, 30 sheets
- Big Time Learning Clock®

Can You Tell Time?

Topic
Reading a digital clock

Key Question
What do the numbers on a digital clock represent?

Learning Goals
Students will:
1. identify the hour and minute positions on a digital clock;
2. set and record digital time using a model digital clock; and
3. determine, through counting-on, the number of minutes left in the hour.

Guiding Document
NCTM Standards 2000*
- *Recognize the attributes of length, volume, weight, area, and time*
- *Understand how to measure using nonstandard and standard units*

Math
Measurement
  time

Integrated Processes
Observing
Comparing and contrasting
Relating

Materials
For each student:
  container with a 24-cm circumference (see *Management 1*)
  transparent tape
  number strips (see *Management 2*)
  Digital Clock Face (see *Management 2*)
  scratch paper
  student recording sheet

For the class:
  digital demonstration clock
    (see *Management 2*)
  overhead transparency of *Digital Time*
  overhead marking pens, red and blue
  utility knife

Management
1. Potato chip cans or containers used to package tennis balls work well for this activity. If you choose to use a container with a larger circumference,

such as a two-liter bottle, extend the length of the number strips to wrap around the container.
2. Construct a digital demonstration clock by cutting out one copy of the *Digital Clock Face* (copied on card stock), one set of the hour number strips, and one set of the minute strips. To continue the color coding for minutes and hours, copy the first page of number strips on red paper and the second page of number strips on blue paper. Using a craft knife, cut the openings on the *Digital Clock Face* for the number strips. Weave the strips through the slots, wrap them around the can, and tape them together. Set the time to read 1:00.

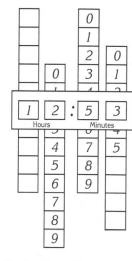 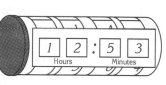

3. In *Part Two,* each student will need their own model digital clock. Prepare the number strips and clock faces beforehand so that students do not have to do any cutting. When cutting the number strips, cut to the end of the paper on one end to allow for a tab to overlap.
4. Make an overhead transparency of *Digital Time,* for use in *Part Two*. Record hours in red and minutes in blue.
5. Each student will need a student recording sheet.

Procedure
Part One
1. Set the digital demonstration clock to 1:00. Discuss the color connection to the hours and minutes on the analog clock. Explain that the digital clock is another tool that measures the passing of time. Tell students that the two positions to the left of the colon represent the hours, and the two positions to the right of the colon represent the minutes. Show the students that both *hours* and *minutes* are labeled on the model digital clock to remind them.

2. Show the students that the demonstration clock is set at 1:00. Ask what they think the digital model clock will look like after one minute has passed.

3. Ask the students how long they think a minute is, and how many times they think they could write their names in one minute.

4. Tell the students that you will time them for one minute. Ask them to write their names on scratch paper as many times as possible in that minute. Begin to time the students, and as you do, slowly change the time on the digital clock to show 1:01. At the end of one minute, discuss the number of times the students were able to write their names and whether it seemed like a long time or a short time had passed.

5. Draw attention to the new time on the digital clock. Tell the students that the time is read as "one-o-one," and that it shows that one minute has passed since 1:00. Explain that the minute positions show how many minutes it is after the hour.

6. Ask the students what the clock would look like if another minute passed. Invite a student to set the digital clock to show that two minutes have passed since 1:00. Assist the students in reading the time as "one-o-two," or two minutes after one. Continue this process until the model clock shows 1:09.

7. Ask the students how 1:10 would look on the digital clock. Set the model clock to show 1:10. Read the time, one-ten, or ten minutes after one. Discuss why there was a zero in the first place to the right of the colon and why it is no longer there.

8. Ask several students to set the digital clock to show different times ranging from 1:10 to 1:59.

9. Ask the students what would happen if the time were 1:59 and another minute passed. With the students, start at 59 and count-on by ones to 60.

10. Set the demonstration clock to show 2:00. Discuss the fact that it is now showing a new hour. Tell the students that there are 60 minutes in an hour and that on the sixtieth minute, the hour must change.

11. Set the model clock to show 2:56. Ask the students what time it is and how many minutes are left in the hour. Assist the students in counting-on to 60 to check their answers. Set the clock at various times and ask the students to read the time and tell how many minutes are left in the hour. Remind students that they can count-on to find out how much time is left in the hour.

12. Set the clock to 12:59 and ask the students what time it would be in one minute. The students may say 13 o'clock. Explain that on this clock there is no 13 o' clock, and that the pattern begins again at 1:00, etc.

Part Two

1. Using the procedure described in *Management 2,* guide the students through the construction of their own model digital clocks.

2. Position the demonstration clock to show 3:20. Ask the students to set their clocks to match the demonstration clock. Have them name the time shown on the clocks.

3. Using red and blue overhead pens, record this time on the *Digital Time* transparency in digital notation. Explain that the first set of two numbers names the hour and the next set names the minutes. The colon is simply used to separate the hour numbers from the minute numbers.

4. Reset the demonstration clock to 5:45 and have students set their clocks to match the demonstration clock. Ask them to name the time on their clocks. Give each student a recording sheet. Record the time on the overhead *Digital Time* transparency, and ask the students to do the same on their own mats. Continue this sequence until the students demonstrate an understanding of how to record the time in a digital format.

5. At different times during the day, ask the students to set their clocks to a time you tell them (e.g., Recess is at 10:30.). You may want to set an alarm clock to sound off at different times during the day. When the alarm sounds, ask the students to reset their clocks and the demonstration clock to the correct time. Have them continue to record the digital times on the recording sheet.

Discussion

1. If the clock reads 1:25, what does that mean? [Twenty-five minutes have passed since one o'clock.]

2. If the clock reads 2:58, how much time will have to pass before it is 3:00? [two minutes]

3. What do the two numbers to the left of the colon on a digital clock represent? ...to the right of the colon? [Hours are represented to the left of the colon and minutes are represented to the right of the colon.]

4. What would two-thirty look like on a digital clock? [2:30]

5. What happens on a digital clock one minute after the fifty-ninth minute past the hour? [The hour changes, it becomes the next o'clock.]

6. Show five o'clock on an analog clock. Write the digital time.

IT'S ABOUT TIME!

Evidence of Learning

1. Listen for accuracy as the students identify the hour and minute positions on a digital clock.
2. Look and listen for accuracy as the students read and set their model digital clocks.
3. Listen for accuracy as the students count-on to determine the number of minutes left in the hour.
4. Check for accuracy as the students record digital time on their recording sheet.

Curriculum Correlation

Literature
Slater, Teddy. *Just a Minute (Hello Math Reader Level 2)*. Scholastic, Inc. New York. 1996. (A young boy learns how important it is to know just how long a minute is.)

Digital Clock Face

——— ——— | ——— ———

Hours   Minutes

——— ——— | ——— ———

Hours   Minutes

——— ——— | ——— ———

Hours   Minutes

——— ——— | ——— ———

Hours   Minutes

Hour Strips (red)

	0		0		0
	1		1		1
	2		2		2
	3		3		3
	4		4		4
1	5	1	5	1	5
	6		6		6
	7		7		7
	8		8		8
	9		9		9

Minute Strips (blue)

0	0	0	0	0	0
1	1	1	1	1	1
2	2	2	2	2	2
3	3	3	3	3	3
4	4	4	4	4	4
5	5	5	5	5	5
	6		6		6
	7		7		7
	8		8		6
	9		9		5

Can You Tell Time? Recording Sheet

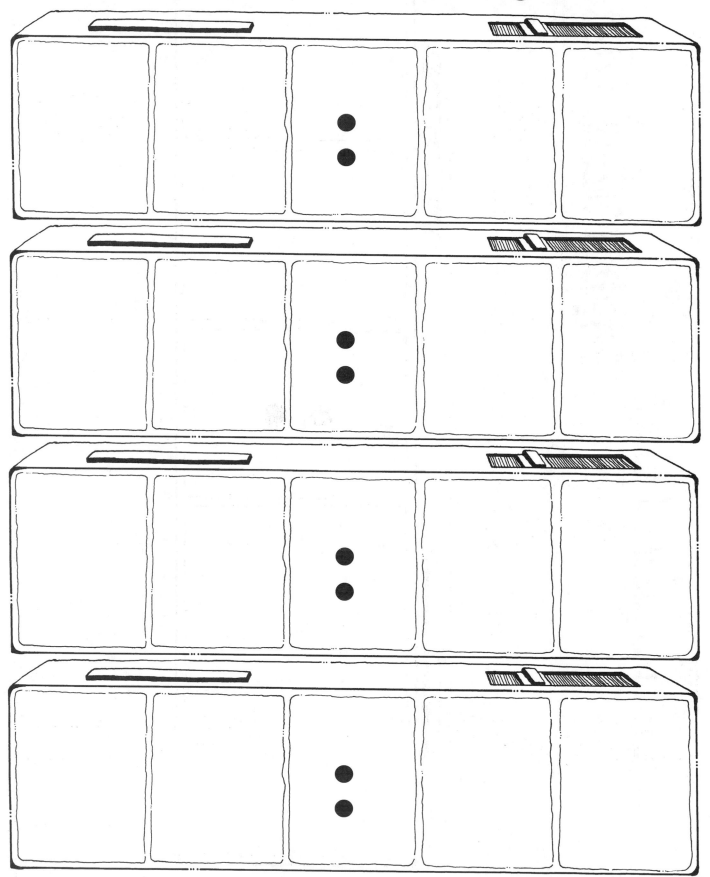

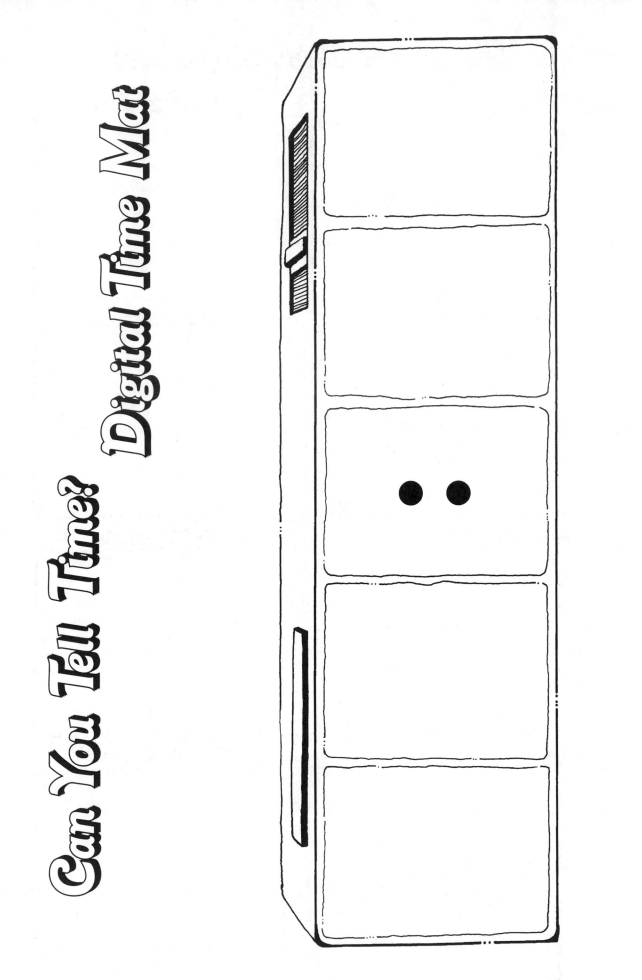

Can You Tell Time?

Digital Time Mat

Flipping Over Time

Topic
Digital and analog clocks

Key Question
How can we compare analog and digital recordings of time using model clocks?

Learning Goal
Students will use student-sized digital and analog clocks to show the relationship between the two.

Guiding Document
NCTM Standards 2000*
- *Recognize the attributes of length, volume, weight, area, and time*
- *Use tools to measure*

Math
Measurement
    time

Integrated Processes
Observing
Comparing and contrasting
Relating

Materials
Card stock numbers (see *Management 1*)
Binder rings and dowels (see *Management 2*)
Student clocks (see *Management 3*)

Management
1. On 8 $\frac{1}{2}$- x 11-inch card stock, make two sets of numbers from zero to 9, one set of numbers from zero to five, one set with the digit 1 and a blank card, and one colon symbol. It is suggested that you continue the color-coding established in previous lessons, using blue for the numbers representing the minutes and red for the numbers representing the hours (see *Procedure 2*).
2. Gather ten binder rings and five dowels. Use a hole punch to make holes at the top of the number

cards. Attach two binder rings to each card set. Insert a dowel through the rings so the number cards can be flipped.
3. Use the paper plate student clocks made in previous activities or the Big Time Learning Clocks®.

Procedure
1. Gather the entire class with their student clocks.
2. Give each of five children a set of the cards and have them arrange themselves in a straight line from left to right:
   - the first child has a red set of cards with the digit one and a blank card,
   - the second child holds a set of red zero to nine cards,
   - the third child holds the colon symbol,
   - the fourth holds a set of blue cards from zero to five, and
   - the fifth child holds a set of blue zero to nine cards.
3. Ask each of the children holding number cards on a ring to flip to a number. Ask the class to read the time on the model clock. Continue to ask students in the class to set the student digital clock to represent a variety of times.
4. Ask the *Key Question*.
5. Have the class set their analog paper plate clocks to a specific time. Ask a student to set the student digital clock to represent the same time. Discuss the relationship between the two recordings of the time.
6. Continue to compare analog and digital times as described above.
7. Have the class set their analog clocks to show their bedtime. Have the five children display a bedtime with the digits on the rings. Ask the children if there are any matches.
8. Repeat the activity by asking when their favorite cartoon is on or when they eat dinner.
9. Set a time with the numbers on the rings and ask the class to set their analog clocks one hour later or earlier.

Discussion
1. What numbers would a digital clock display at 12 o'clock? [12:00]
2. Name a time and flip the cards to match.
3. If the digital clock shows 2:35, what number(s) represent the hour? ...the minutes? [2,35]
4. If the digital clock shows 11:58, how many flips will it be until 12:00? [two]

5. What type of clock do you think is easier to read, a digital clock or an analog clock? Why?

Evidence of Learning
Look for accuracy in the displays on both the student digital and analog clocks.

Extension
Set up a concentration game with digital times on cards and matching clock faces on another set of cards.

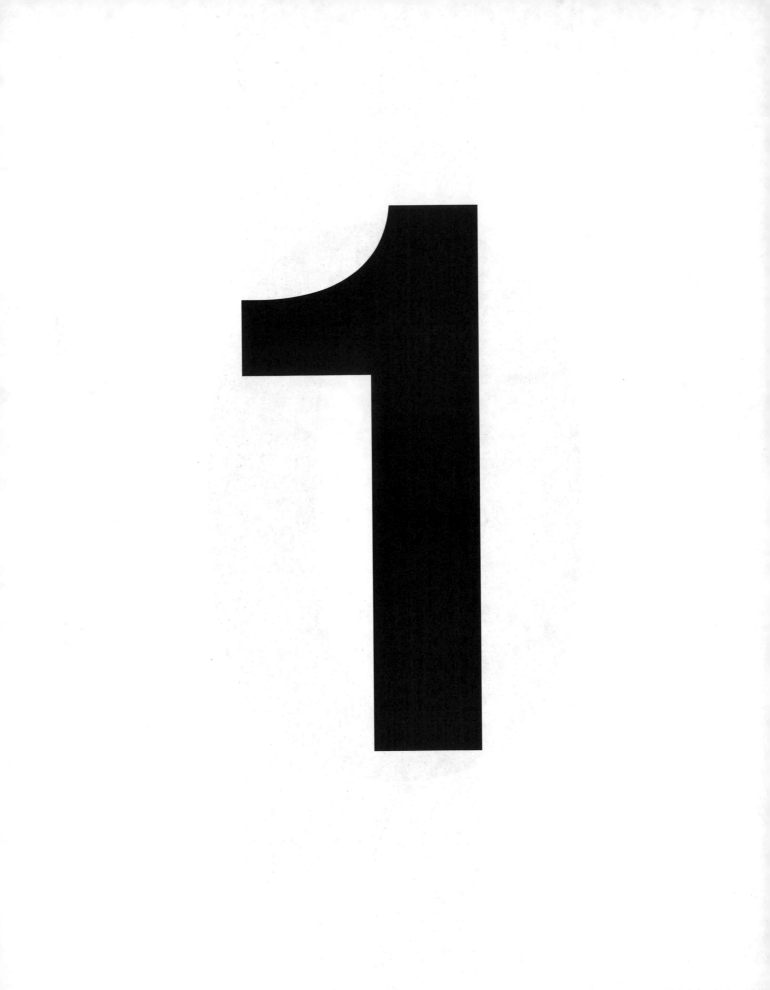

61

64

65

67

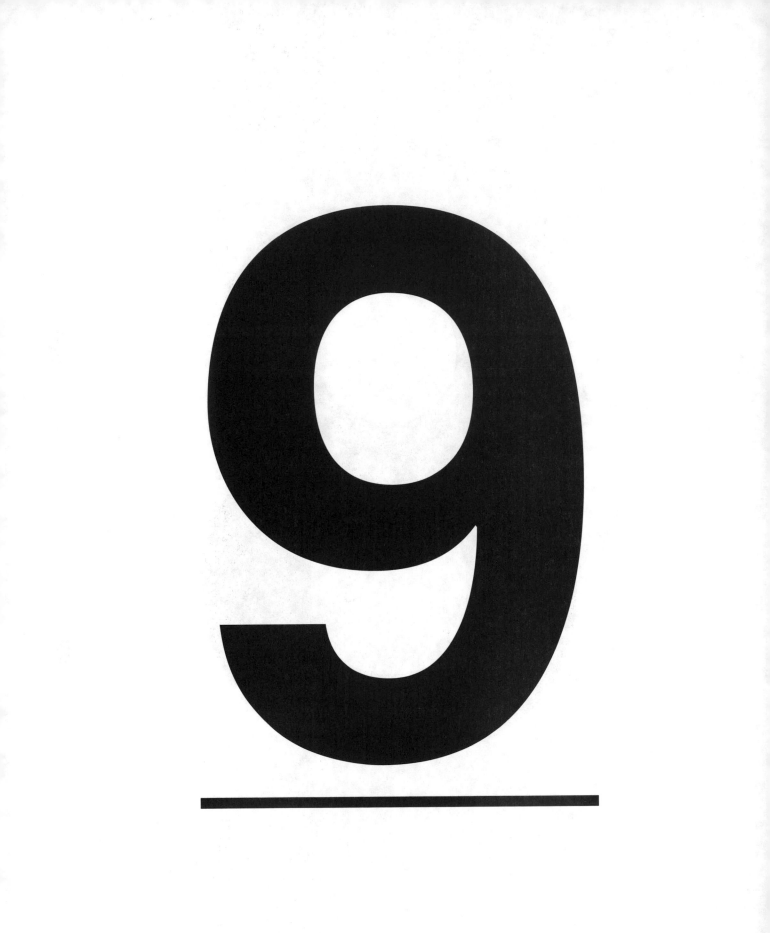

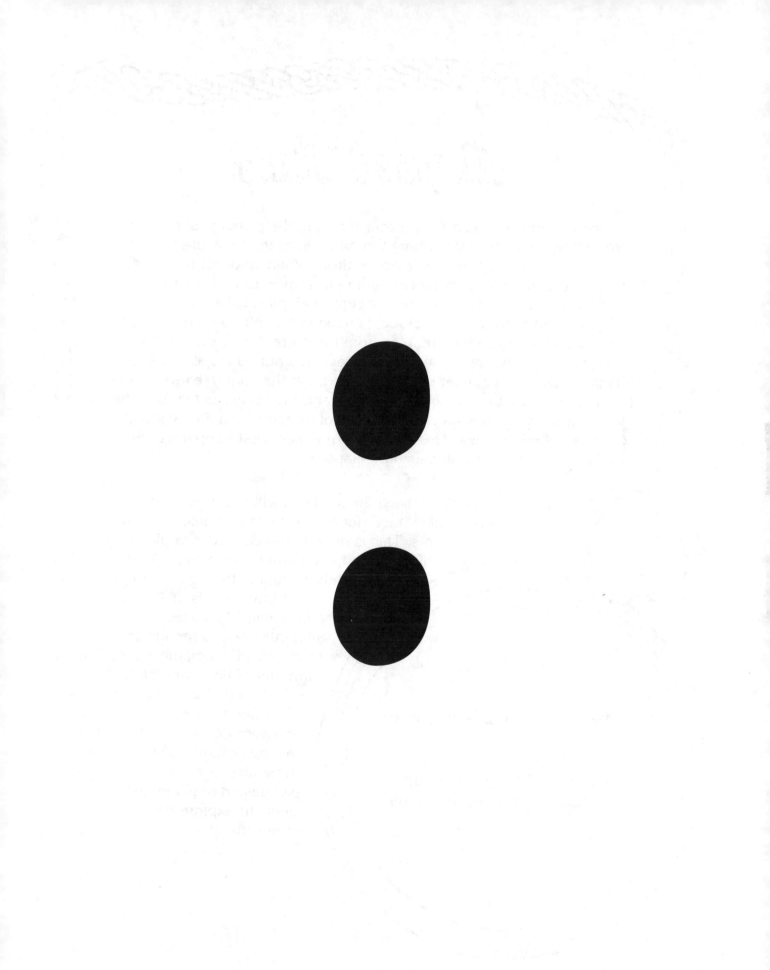

Elapsed Time

Clocks and watches are tools that measure the passage of time in formal units. The amount of time that passes, or the measured duration of an event, is considered the elapsed time. When students have a good grasp of the mechanics of clock reading it is important for them to develop an understanding of the concept of elapsed time.

By the end of third grade, students need to be able to mentally add or subtract the number of minutes from the current time on the clock to determine the amount of time that has elapsed during a specific event. It is important for younger students to begin at the concrete level. Have them identify the beginning time of an event, then physically move the clock hands forward a specified number of minutes, and finally identify the time the event ends. This allows them to see what happens to the hands of the clock or watch as time elapses.

In the following activity, the students will use model clocks and watches to determine the amount of time that elapses between specific events. This is done in the context of a playful game format and a literature connection. Attention should be given to changing the hour hand position as well as the minute hands as they use their Big Time Learning Clocks®.

Students need to recognize how elapsed time can influence their daily lives. The amount of time that it takes them to get ready for school affects the time that they get up. The effects of overcooking or undercooking food are real examples of how elapsed time affects our lives. A page of suggested applications for the students to explore follows the elapsed time activity.

Materials for this section:

- Small paper bag
- Blue and red masking tape
- Paper clips, large and small

Watch the Time Fly

Topic
Elapsed time

Key Question
What happens to the hands of a watch or clock as time passes?

Learning Goal
Students will use model watches to record the passing of time.

Guiding Document
NCTM Standards 2000*
- *Recognize the attributes of length, volume, weight, area, and time*
- *Understand how to measure using nonstandard and standard units*
- *Use tools to measure*

Math
Measurement
    time

Integrated Processes
Observing
Comparing and contrasting
Applying
Relating

Materials
For the class:
    small paper bag
    elapsed time cards (see *Management 3*)
    blue and red tape
    transparent tape

For each student:
    two paper clips, one large and one small
    student book
    brass paper fastener
    pocket watch
    recording page
    2 ft. string or paper clip chain made of 10 small
       paper clips

Management
1. Prior to this lesson make copies of the student book, *A Day for Friends,* for each child. Each student will also need a

pocket watch copied onto card stock. Students may need some assistance in assembling the book and making the pocket watch.

2. Before beginning this lesson, wrap one large paper clip with blue tape and one small paper clip with red tape for each pocket watch. The colored tape will connect the student model to commercial educational clock models.

3. Make two copies of *Elapsed Time Cards* on card stock for each group of four students. Two sets of cards, five-minute interval cards and one-minute interval cards, have been provided. This will allow you to vary the level of difficulty.

Procedure
Part One
1. Read aloud the story at the end of the teacher's text about Nick and Miguel's day.
2. Ask the *Key Question.* Discuss how the hands move clockwise on a clock or watch as time passes. Discuss elapsed time, or the measured duration of an event.
3. Tell the students that they will use a model pocket watch to help Miguel and Nick keep a record of their day.
4. Distribute a student book, a card stock pocket watch, string or paperclip chain, wrapped paper clips, brass paper fastener, and transparent tape to each student.
5. Have students use transparent tape to tape a pocket onto the front cover of each booklet leaving the top of the pocket open to hold the watch. Attach one end of the string or paper clip chain to the watch and the other end to the inside of the pocket.
6. Assist the students as they insert the paper fastener through the small end of both paper clips and into the center of the watch on the student book.
7. Direct the students to use their model watch to record the passing of time as you read the story together. Explain that they will record the actual time mentioned in each part of the story and the time that elapses between the events.
8. Instruct the students to set their watches to 12:00 since the story begins at noon.
9. After each event in the story, have the students set their watches to correspond with the new time. Discuss the amount of time that elapsed and ask

the students to show their model watches after each event so you can check for accuracy.

10. Have the students record the beginning time, the time elapsed, and the new time in their student books as you read through the story.

Part Two

1. Invite four students to a table.
2. Tell the students that they will be playing a game in which they will be moving the hands of their pocket watch forward to keep track of the elapsed time similar to what they did with the story about Nick and Miguel.
3. Instruct each student to set the hands of his or her watch to show 12:00. Shake the paper bag containing *Elapsed Time Cards* and draw one card out. Show the students the card and tell them to move the hands of their clocks forward that many minutes. Discuss the ending time. Demonstrate how to record their results on the *Watch the Time Fly* recording page.

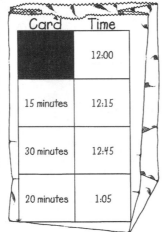

Card	Time
	12:00
15 minutes	12:15
30 minutes	12:45
20 minutes	1:05

4. Explain that they will continue taking turns drawing a card from the bag and moving the hands of their pocket watch forward the number of minutes indicated on the card.
5. Tell the students that the object of the game is to be the first one to reach 6:00. If they run out of cards before anyone reaches 6:00 The winner will be the student(s) that comes closest to 6:00.

Discussion

1. If it is 3:00 and your favorite television show comes on at 5:00, how long will you need to wait to see it? [two hours]
2. If it is 12:00, what time will it be in 15 minutes? [12:15]
3. What is elapsed time?
4. Did the boys in the story spend more time at the park or at Miguel's house? [Miguel's house]
5. How could we solve the problem "It is 2:00, what time was it 30 minutes ago?"

Evidence of Learning

Check for accuracy as students show and record the time that elapses between events.

A Day for Friends

It was noon on a warm summer Saturday. Nick had just finished watching cartoons when his mother sent him outside to get some fresh air. He knew his best friend Miguel would be at school playing basketball at 12:30. How many minutes until Miguel got to school? [30 minutes] He walked to the school and arrived just as Miguel did. They played for an hour. What time was it then? [1:30] Next, the boys decided to go to the park to ride their skateboards. The park was 15 minutes away. When did they arrive at the park? [1:45] They rode their skateboards for half an hour, then decided they would go to Miguel's house to play video games. What time did they leave the park? [2:15] The boys had been playing video games for an hour and 30 minutes when their friend Jalisa came over. What time did Jalisa arrive? [3:45]. She suggested that they all go fishing, so the three friends went down to the creek. They stayed at the creek for an hour. While they were there, they saw three toads, dozens of tadpoles, two birds, a dog, and no fish. What time did they leave the creek? [4:45] By now they were beginning to get hungry. Nick's house was the closest. They knew they could get there in 15 minutes if they ran, so they did. What time did they arrive at Nick's house? [5:00] When the three hungry friends arrived at Nick's house, his mother told them that it was time for their day together to end. It was 5:00 and time for everyone to go home for dinner. The three friends said goodbye and decided to meet at 9:00 on Monday for another day of fun.

A Day for Friends

Book Cover Pockets

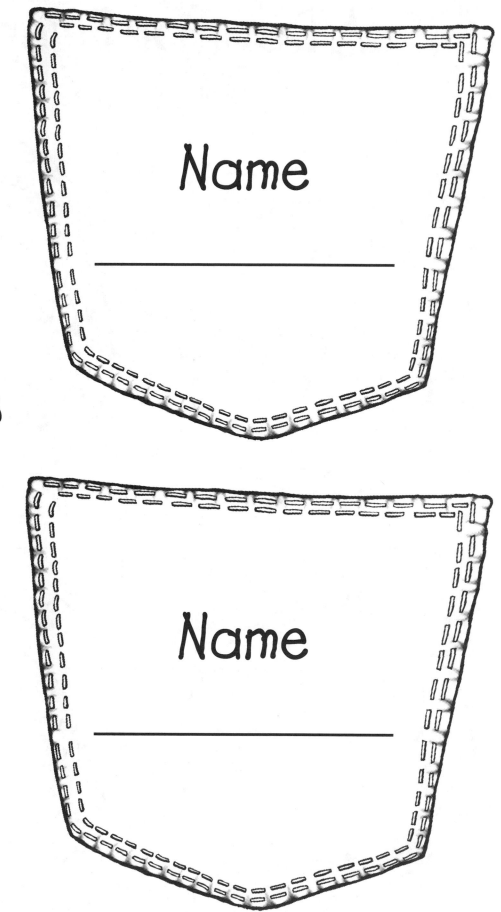

Name

_____

Name

_____

A Day for Friends

Book Watches

A DAY FOR FRIENDS

tape your pocket here

It was noon on a warm summer Saturday.

He knew his best friend Miguel would be at school playing basketball at 12:30.

Nick had just finished watching cartoons when his mother sent him outside to get some fresh air.

How many minutes until Miguel got to school?

_____

Next, the boys decided to go to the park to ride their skateboards. The park was 15 minutes away.

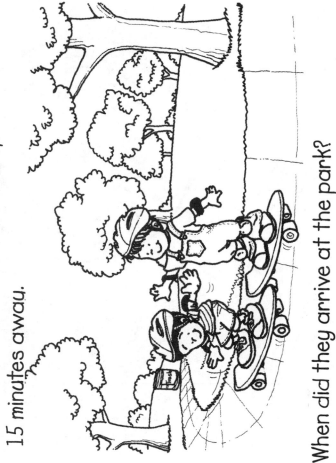

When did they arrive at the park?

4

He walked to the school and arrived just as Miguel did. They played for an hour.

What time was it then?

3

The boys had been playing video games for an hour and 30 minutes when their friend Jalisa came over.

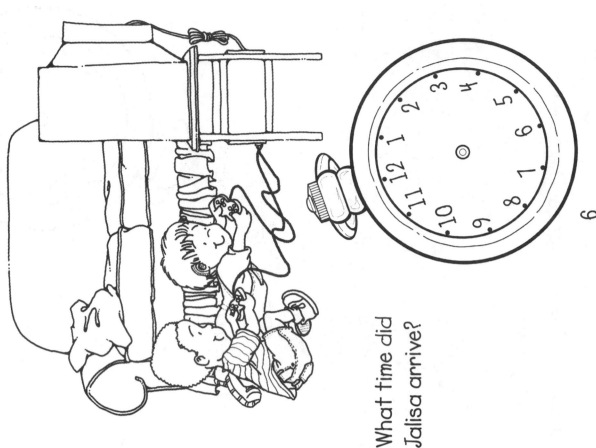

What time did Jalisa arrive?

6

IT'S ABOUT TIME!

They rode their skateboards for half an hour, then decided they would go to Miguel's house to play video games.

What time did they leave the park?

5

IT'S ABOUT TIME!

She suggested that they all go fishing, so the three friends went down to the creek. They stayed at the creek for an hour. While they were there, they saw three toads, dozens of tadpoles, two birds, a dog, and no fish.

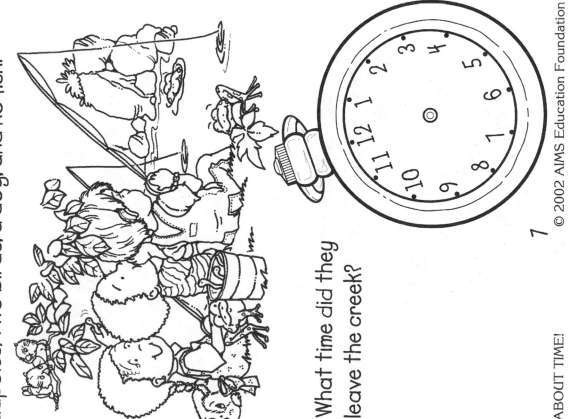

What time did they leave the creek?

7

By now they were beginning to get hungry. Nick's house was the closest. They knew they could get there in 15 minutes if they ran, so they did.

What time did they arrive at Nick's house?

8

When the three hungry friends arrived at Nick's house, his mother told them that it was time for their day together to end. It was 5:00 and time for everyone to go home for dinner. The three friends said goodbye and decided to meet at 9:00 on Monday for another day of fun.

I read my story to these people:

_____

_____

_____

_____

_____

_____

_____

Elapsed Time Cards

What time will it be in 5 minutes?

What time will it be in 15 minutes?

What time will it be in 30 minutes?

What time will it be in 45 minutes?

What time will it be in 60 minutes?

What time will it be in 20 minutes?

What time will it be in 10 minutes?

What time will it be in 35 minutes?

Elapsed Time Cards

What time will it be in 4 minutes?

What time will it be in 8 minutes?

What time will it be in 12 minutes?

What time will it be in 34 minutes?

What time will it be in 42 minutes?

What time will it be in 6 minutes?

What time will it be in 16 minutes?

What time will it be in 24 minutes?

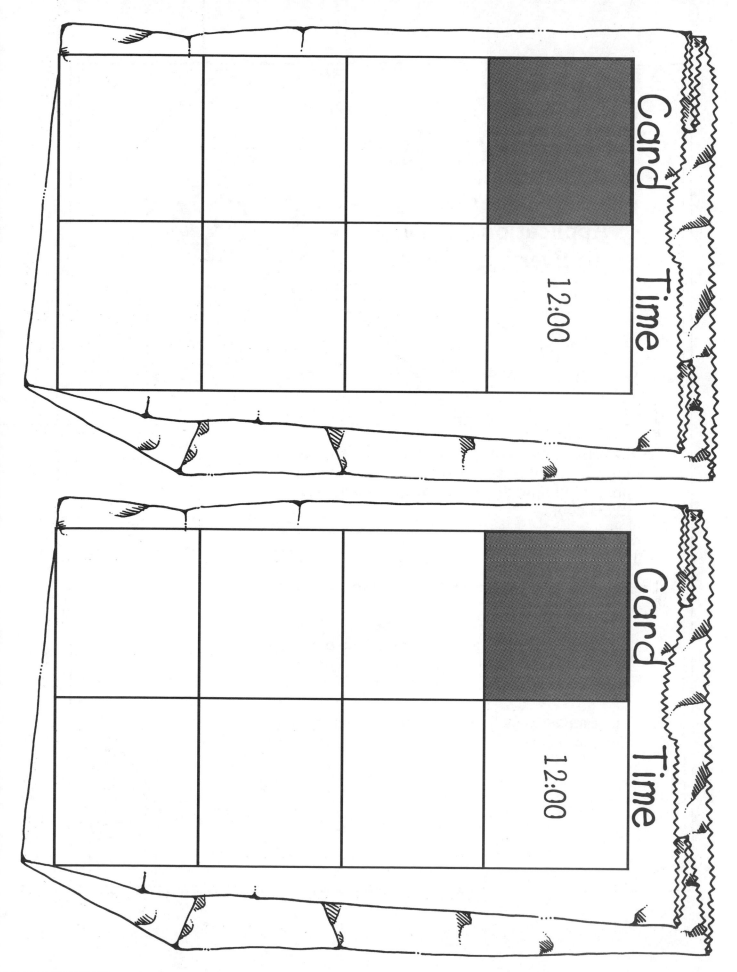

Card Time

12:00

Card Time

12:00

Time Matters

Suggested Applications of Time to Everyday Events

- Experiment with overcooking and undercooking cupcakes, toast, etc. Determine the optimum amount of time that should elapse while these items cook.

- Time students as they run the 100-yard dash.

- See how far students can run in 60 seconds.

- Make juice pops, observing them every 30 minutes until students have determined the optimum freezing time. Discuss what happens if enough time does not elapse before they try to eat them.

- Time students as they take turns at centers or on the computer.

Playful and Intelligent Practice

The practice provided in this section focuses on clock reading; however, students should be able to provide evidence that shows an understanding of the concepts of time before they are moved to the mechanics of using analog and digital clocks. Since clock reading is a skill that is used in everyday life, telling time is something that should be practiced daily. The following activities were designed to be used over and over for continued practice in identifying various representations of selected times.

Materials for this section:

- Game cards (patterns included)
- Game board (pattern included)
- Math chips
- Scissors
- Glue

Triple Time

Purpose of the Game
Students will practice reading analog clocks, digital clocks, and time words.

Materials
Set of *Triple Time* Cards (see *Management* 1)

Management
1. Copy a set of *Triple Time* Cards onto card stock. Each group will need one set.
2. This card game works best when played in a group of two to four students.

Rules for Game One
This game is a version of *Go Fish* using time. A *Triple Time* set is a set of three cards with the same time listed in analog, digital, and time words. The object of the game is to collect as many *Triple Time* sets as possible.

1. One player begins by shuffling the cards and dealing seven to each player.
2. The player to the left of the dealer begins by asking another player for a time that will match a card in his or her hand. For example, "Do you have 12:00?"
3. If the player asked has any cards that correspond to the requested time, he/she must surrender those cards to the player who requested them, and that player's turn continues.
4. If the player asked does not have any cards that correspond to the requested time, the player who asked must draw a card, and his/her turn is over. Play then continues in a clockwise direction.
5. As soon as any player gets all three cards in a *Triple Time* set, the cards are to be placed on the table and are no longer in play.
6. The game ends when one player runs out of cards.
7. The winner is the player with the most *Triple Time* sets.

Rules for Game Two
This game is a version of *Memory* using time. Use the cards from *Triple Time*. The object of the game is to collect as many *Triple Time* sets as possible.
1. Select 12 sets of three cards each from the deck. There will be 36 cards in all.
2. Arrange the cards in a pocket chart so that they form a six by six array. Label the vertical columns with the numbers one through six, and the horizontal rows with the letters A through F.

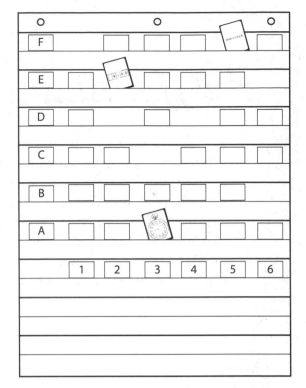

3. Divide the class into two teams.
4. Have one team begin by asking you to flip three cards using the coordinates established. For example: 3A, 2E, and 5F.
5. If those three cards are a set, they are removed from the chart and given to that team, and that team's turn continues. If they are not a *Triple Time* set, play moves to the other team.
6. Play continues until all the sets have been claimed.
7. The winner is the team with the most sets.
8. After playing this game as a class, students can play with a partner or in small groups on the floor.

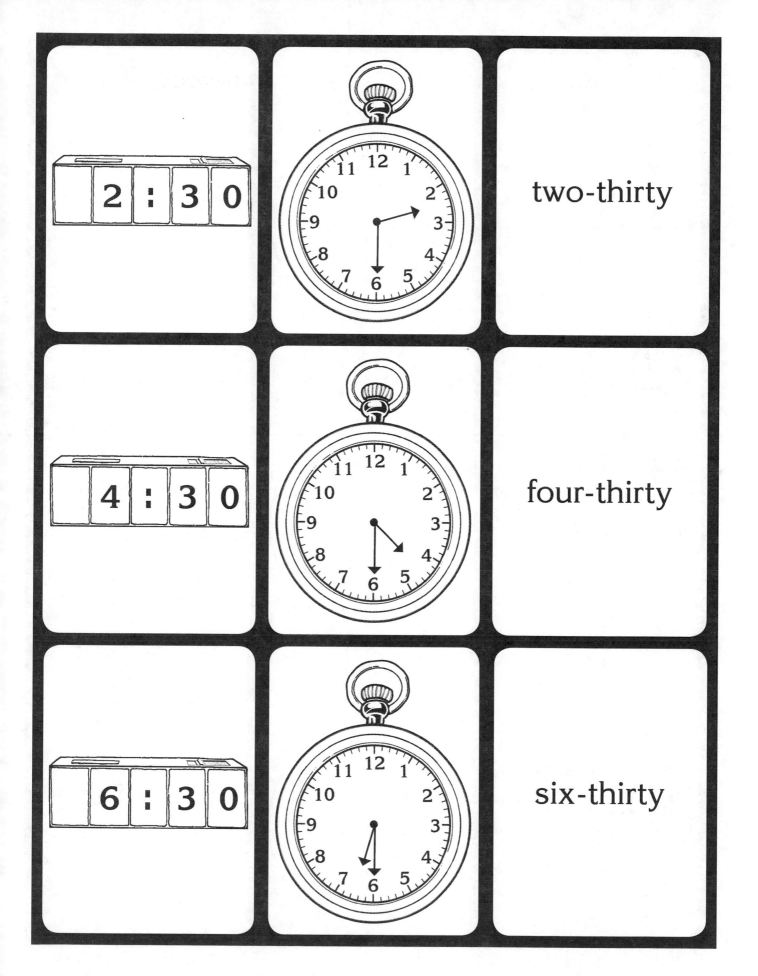

2:30   two-thirty

4:30   four-thirty

6:30   six-thirty

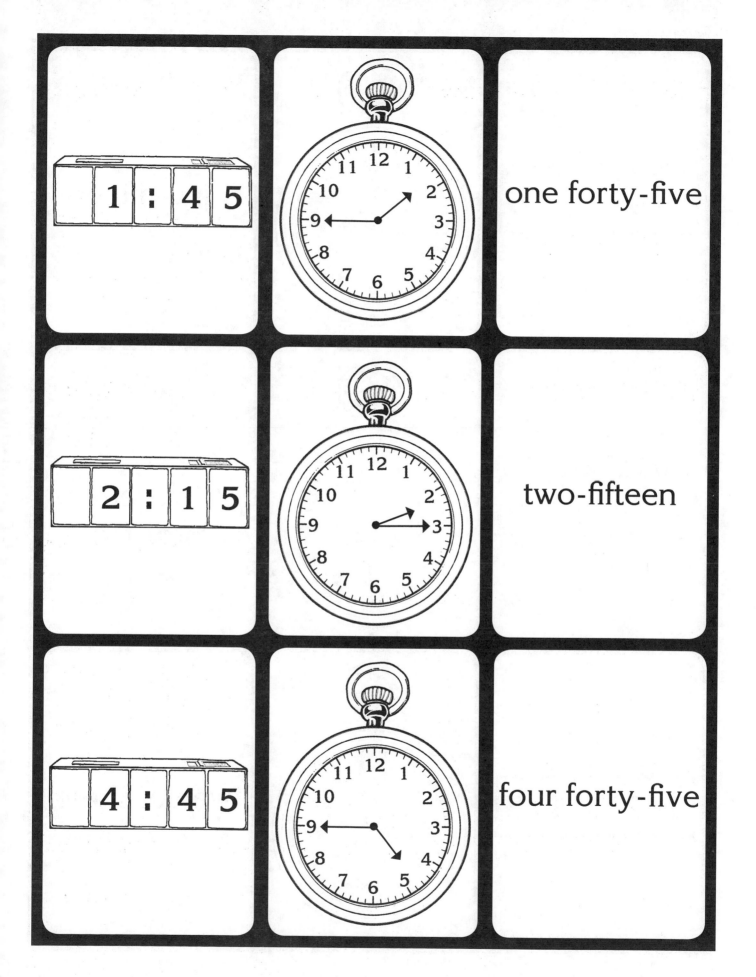

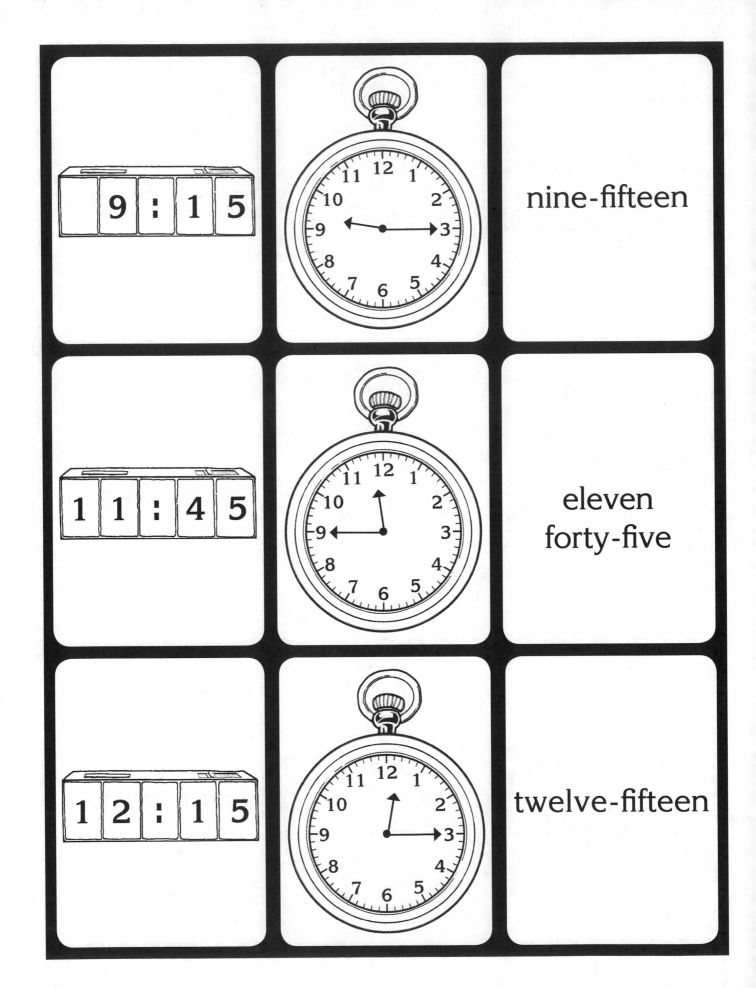

Time Travels

Purpose of the Game
Students will practice reading analog and digital clocks.

Materials
Large set of clocks (see *Management 1*)

Management
1. Copy the analog and digital clocks onto card stock and laminate for durability.
2. Prepare at least one clock for each student in the class.

Rules
1. Gather students into a circle. Give each student a clock. Direct the students to place their clocks at their feet on the floor.
2. Ask one student at a time to read the time on the clock at his or her feet.
3. Have students turn so that they are facing the back of the person in front of them. As in school carnival cake walks, start some music and have the students slowly walk around the circle until you stop the music.

4. When the music stops, tell the children to stop as well. Tell the students who are standing next to 12:00 to hop on one foot. Then tell the students who are standing next to 12:30 to turn around.
5. Have the students return to their walking positions and start the music again. Continue stopping the music and giving movement directions for the different times as before until all times have been called and all children have had an opportunity to read a clock and respond with the appropriate movement.

Discussion
1. What does 12:30 look like on an analog clock? ...a digital clock?
2. What do the two numbers to the right of the colon on a digital clock represent? [the minutes]
3. Would you rather read an analog clock or a digital clock? Why?
4. Which times where easier to read? Explain your thinking.
5. How are the two types of clocks similar? How are they different?

Extension
Turn the clocks over and play the memory game. Have the students locate the person that has a clock with the same time displayed as on their clock.

The following times are given in both analog and digital format:

12:00
12:15
8:00
9:00
3:15
9:25
9:30
10:30
2:30
7:45
6:35
5:40
1:10
2:20
7:50

108

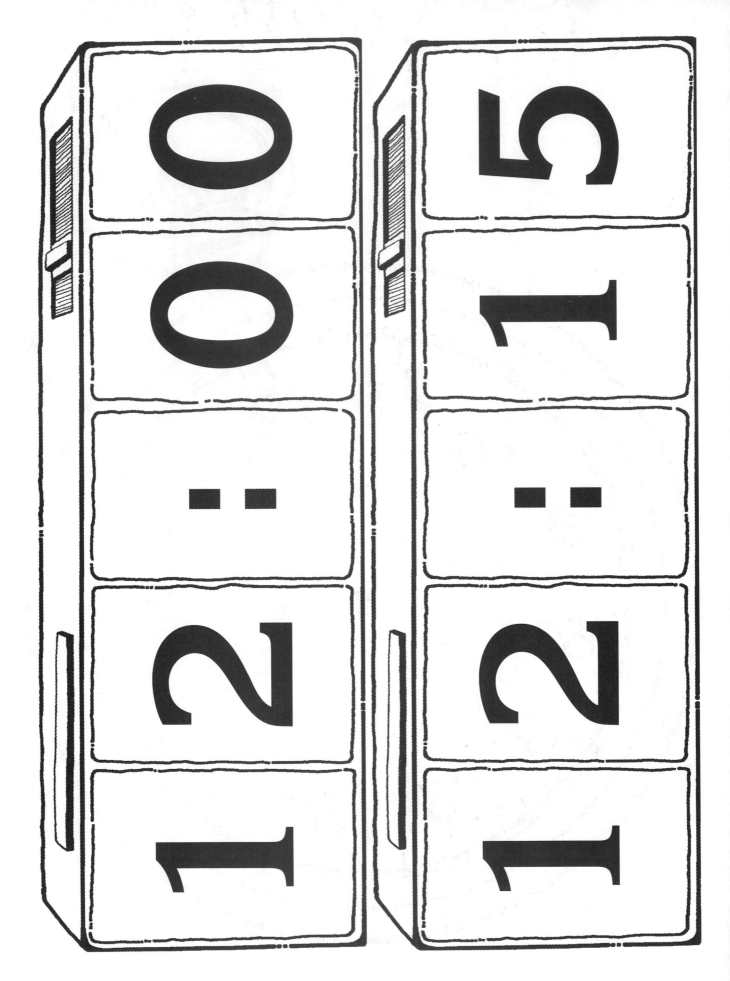

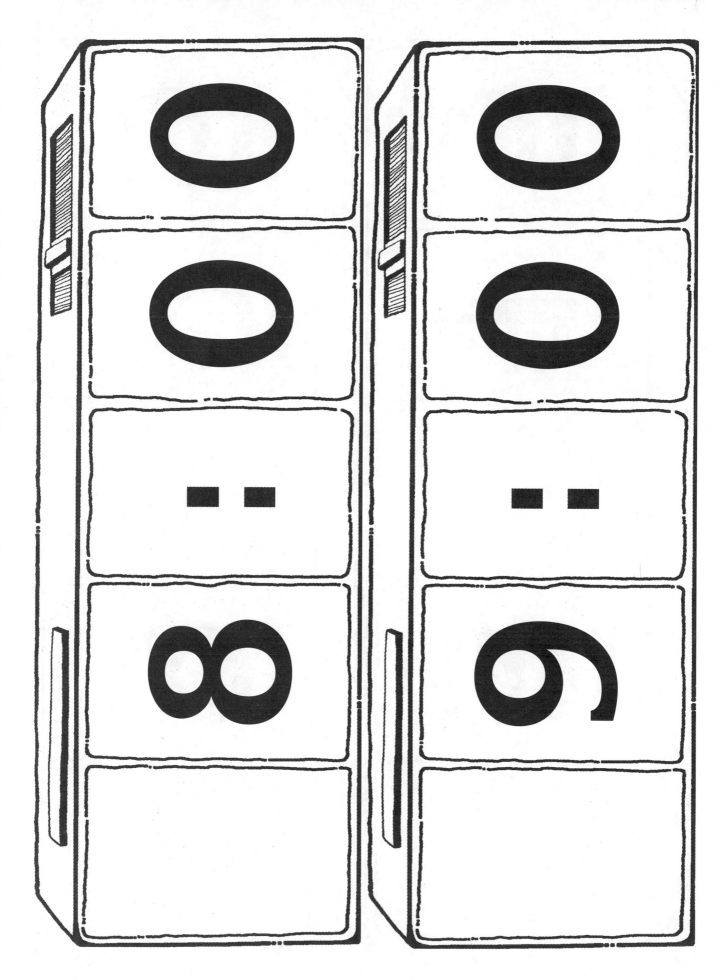

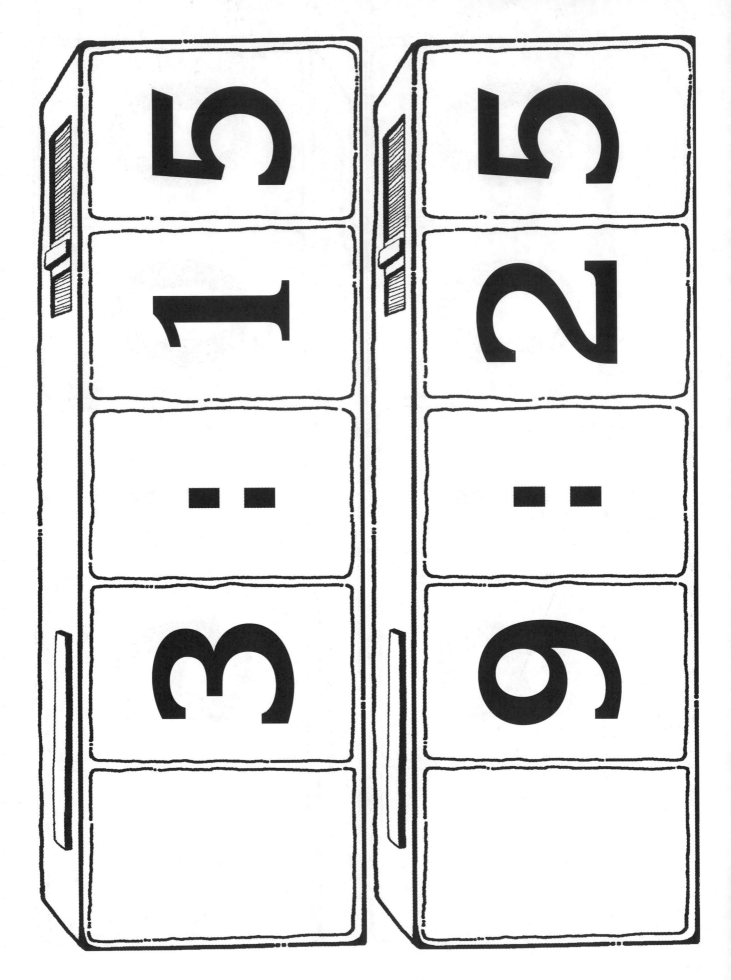

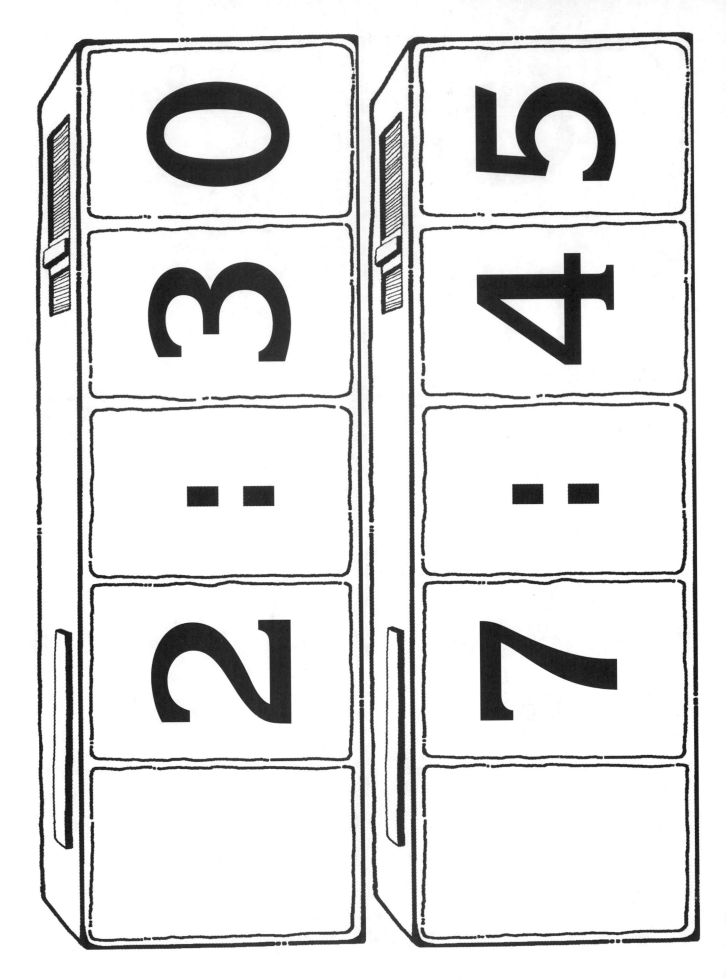

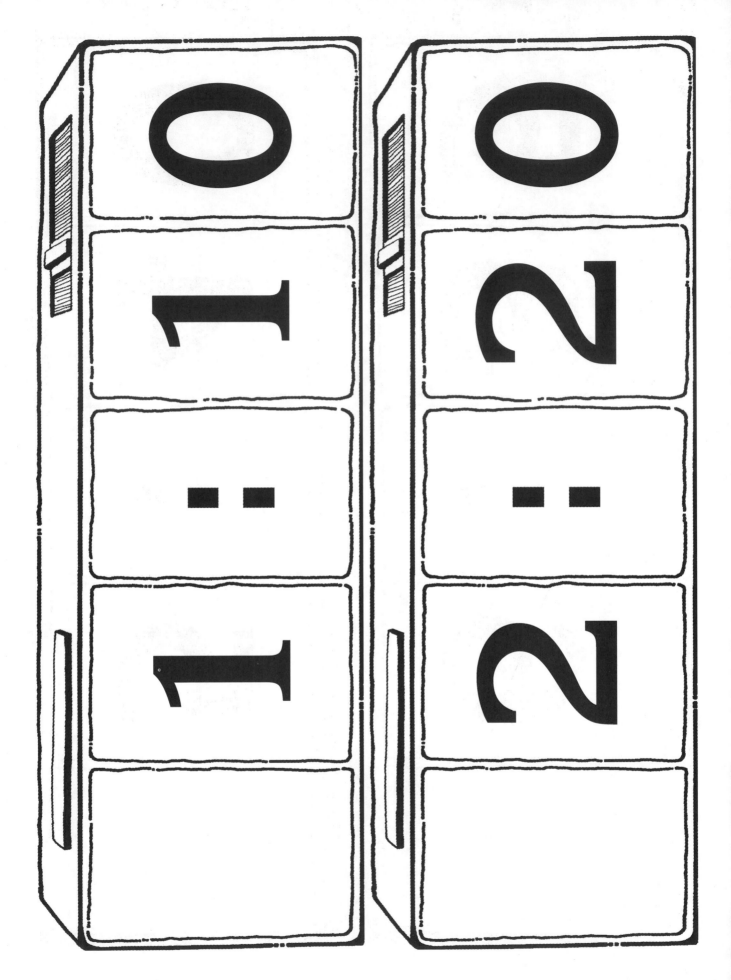

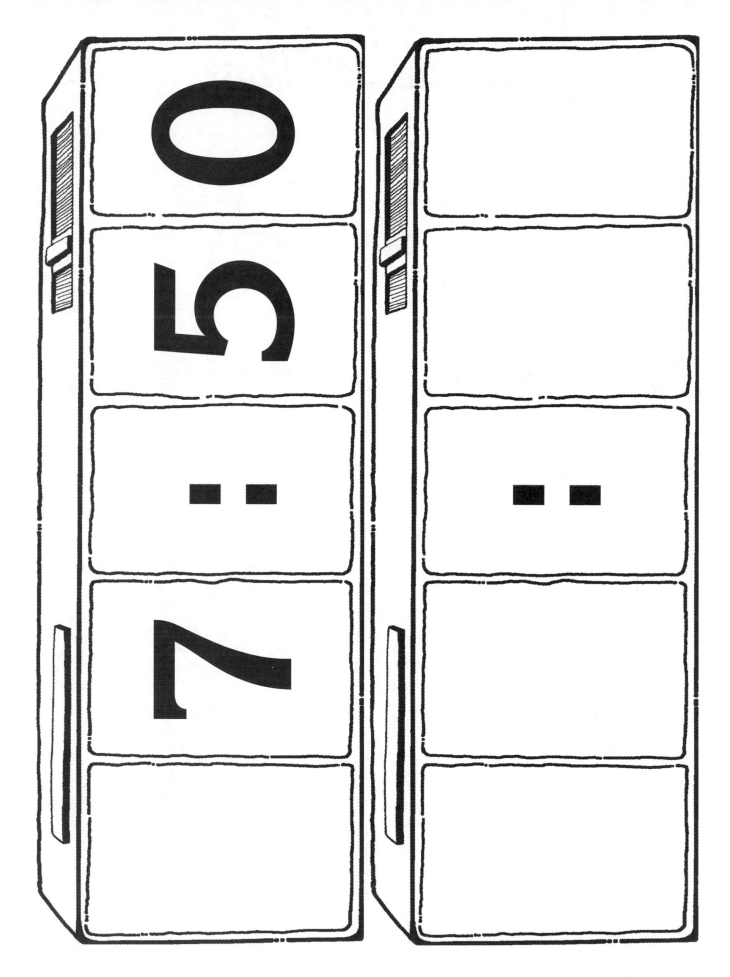

Who Has? Time

Primary students benefit from revisiting basic skills through repeated experiences in a variety of formats. While the adage *practice makes perfect* makes sense to us, there is considerable support for the idea that "drilling" for periods longer than 10 minutes a day may be counterproductive.

This learning game provides playful and intelligent practice within a very short period of time. The game features:

- an element of "playfulness,"
- minimum teacher preparation,
- time efficiency,
- mental stimulation and exercise,
- student interest and motivation, and
- 100 percent accuracy.

Management

1. Two experiences have been provided to allow for different ability levels. *Set One* deals with hours and half-hours. *Set Two* deals with five-minute readings.
2. Copy the clocks or watches onto card stock and laminate for extended use.
3. Cut them out for distribution.
4. Students can wear the watches if brass paper fasteners are placed on both ends of the watchbands and rubber bands are used to connect the two fasteners.

Procedure

1. Distribute one clock or watch to each student or pair of students.
2. Begin with any clock or watch.
3. Begin the game by reading the time on a clock or watch aloud. For example, "I have 1:25. Who has 6:55?"
4. Direct the student holding the clock or watch with that time to respond by saying what time is on his or her clock(watch). For example, "I have 6:55. Who has 8:25?"
5. Continue the game until the cycle returns to the beginning clock or watch.

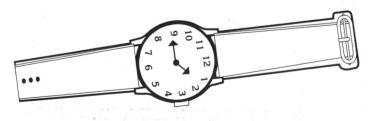

Who Has? Time Time Key (Set One—Clocks)

1. I have 1:00. Who has 2:30?
2. I have 2:30. Who has 12:00?
3. I have 12:00. Who has 11:30?
4. I have 11:30. Who has 11:00?
5. I have 11:00. Who has 2:00?
6. I have 2:00. Who has 12:30?
7. I have 12:30. Who has 9:00?
8. I have 9:00. Who has 1:30?
9. I have 1:30. Who has 3:00?
10. I have 3:00. Who has 8:00?
11. I have 8:00. Who has 6:30?
12. I have 6:30. Who has 4:00?
13. I have 4:00. Who has 7:30?
14. I have 7:30. Who has 10:00?
15. I have 10:00. Who has 3:30?
16. I have 3:30. Who has 7:00?
17. I have 7:00. Who has 9:30?
18. I have 9:30. Who has 5:00?
19. I have 5:00. Who has 4:30?
20. I have 4:30. Who has 10:30?
21. I have 10:30. Who has 6:00?
22. I have 6:00. Who has 8:30?
23. I have 8:30. Who has 5:30?
24. I have 5:30. Who has 1:00?

Who Has? Time Key (Set Two—Watches)

1. I have 1:25. Who has 6:55?
2. I have 6:55. Who has 8:25?
3. I have 8:25. Who has 9:15?
4. I have 9:15. Who has 11:05?
5. I have 11:05. Who has 2:00?
6. I have 2:00. Who has 12:15?
7. I have 12:15. Who has 1:00?
8. I have 1:00. Who has 12:30?
9. I have 12:30. Who has 2:20?
10. I have 2:20. Who has 8:00?
11. I have 8:00. Who has 6:30?
12. I have 6:30. Who has 4:15?
13. I have 4:15. Who has 2:30?
14. I have 2:30. Who has 5:50?
15. I have 5:50. Who has 2:45?
16. I have 2:45. Who has 7:10?
17. I have 7:10. Who has 9:35?
18. I have 9:35. Who has 3:05?
19. I have 3:05. Who has 3:35?
20. I have 3:35. Who has 1:25?

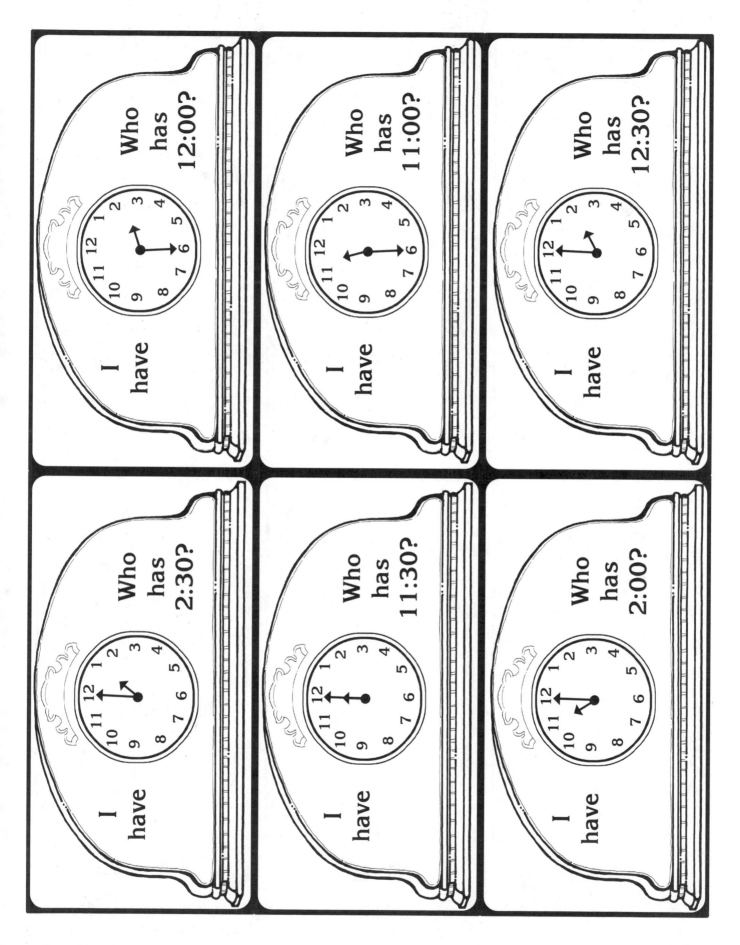

I have

Who has 12:00?

I have

Who has 11:00?

I have

Who has 12:30?

I have

Who has 2:30?

I have

Who has 11:30?

I have

Who has 2:00?

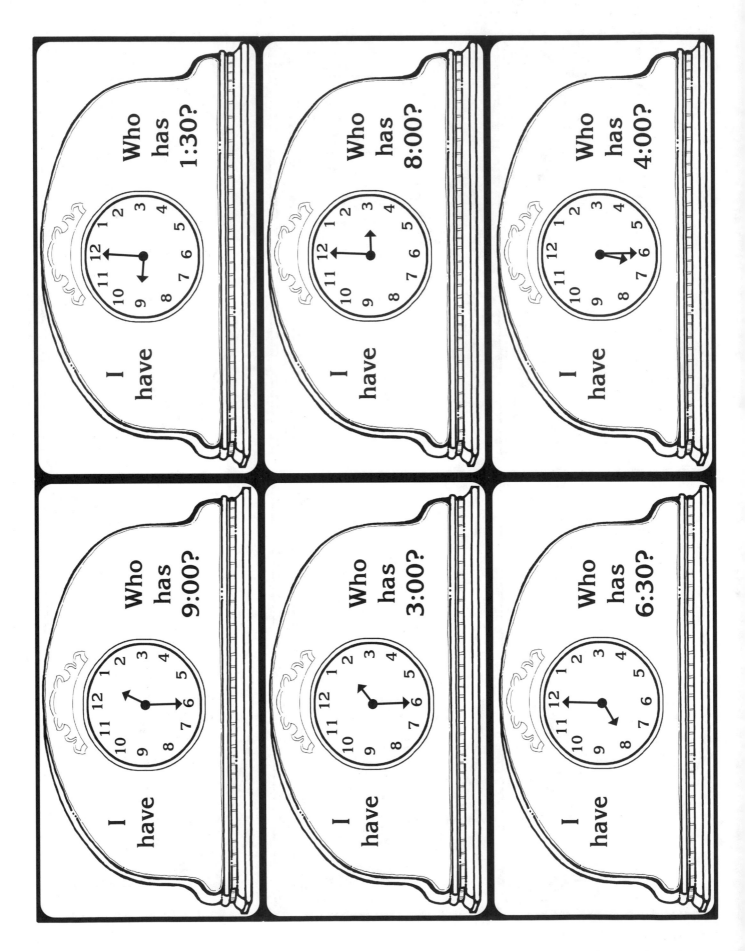

I have | Who has 1:30?

I have | Who has 8:00?

I have | Who has 4:00?

I have | Who has 9:00?

I have | Who has 3:00?

I have | Who has 6:30?

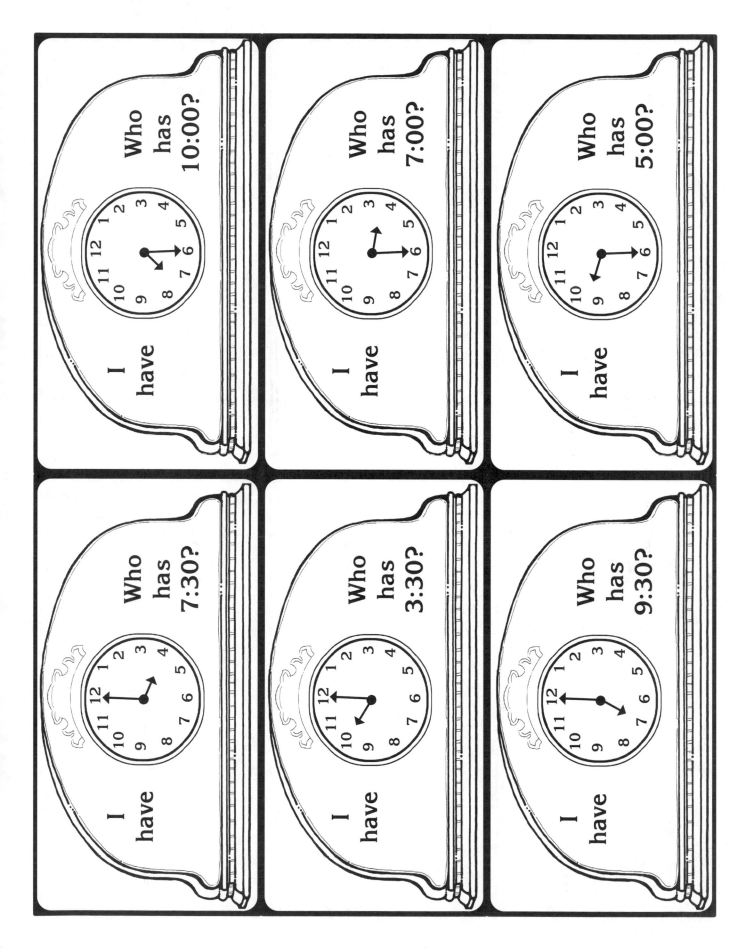

I have

Who has
10:00?

I have

Who has
7:30?

I have

Who has
7:00?

I have

Who has
3:30?

I have

Who has
5:00?

I have

Who has
9:30?

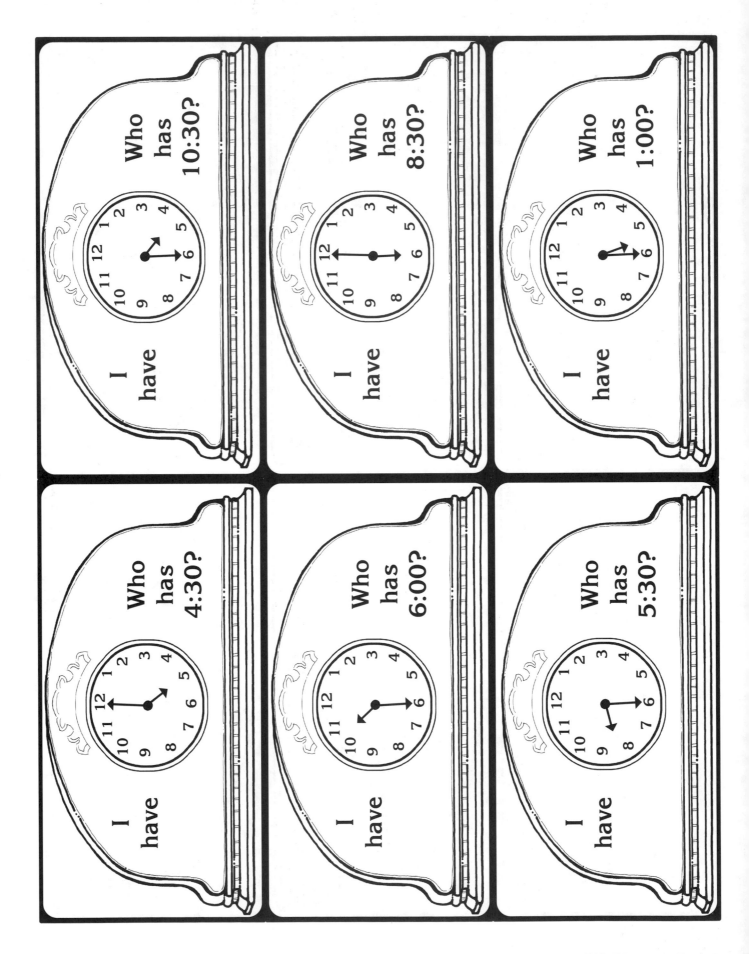

I have / Who has 10:30?

I have / Who has 4:30?

I have / Who has 8:30?

I have / Who has 6:00?

I have / Who has 1:00?

I have / Who has 5:30?

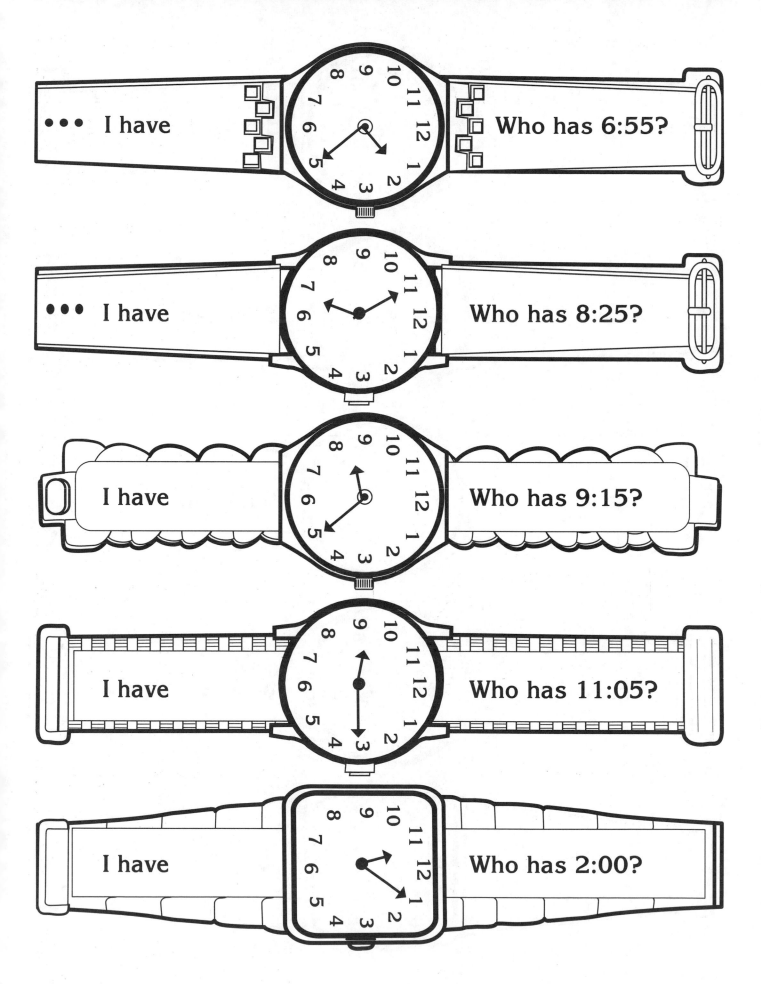

••• I have   Who has 6:55?

••• I have   Who has 8:25?

I have   Who has 9:15?

I have   Who has 11:05?

I have   Who has 2:00?

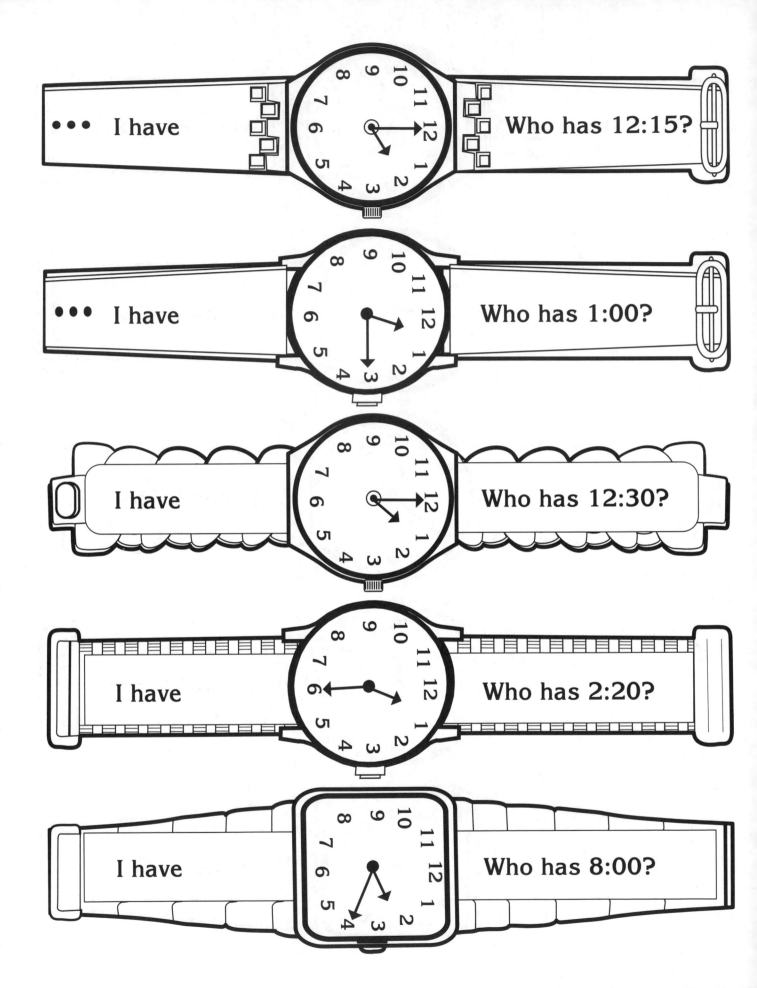

... I have   Who has 12:15?

... I have   Who has 1:00?

I have   Who has 12:30?

I have   Who has 2:20?

I have   Who has 8:00?

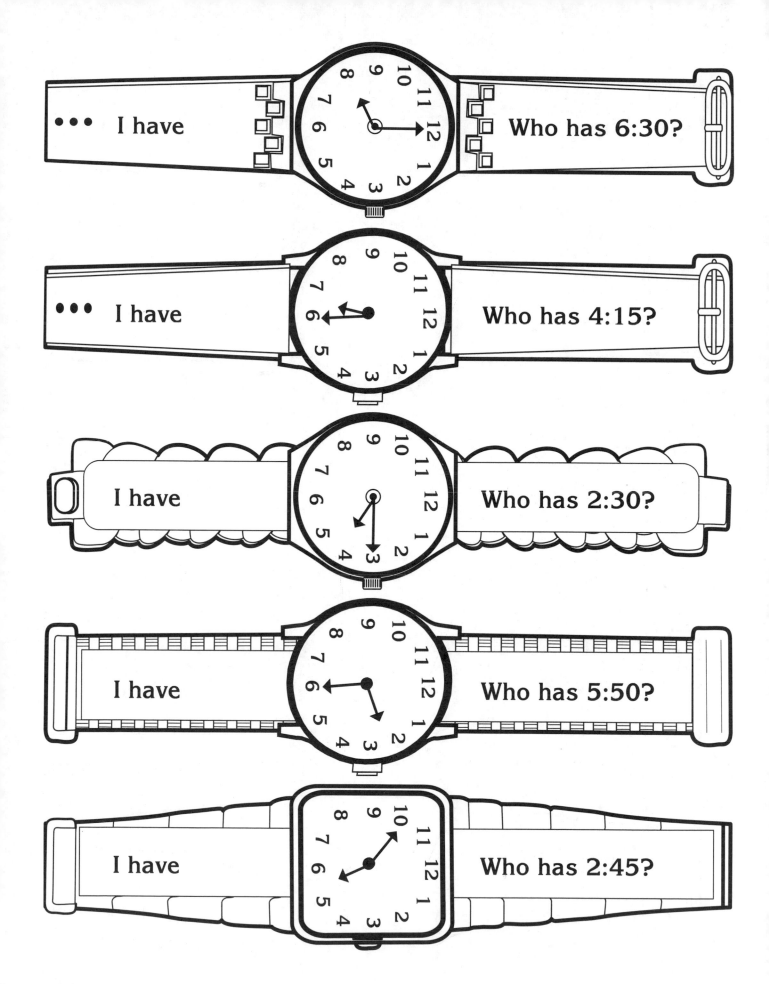

• • • I have   Who has 6:30?

• • • I have   Who has 4:15?

I have   Who has 2:30?

I have   Who has 5:50?

I have   Who has 2:45?

••• I have

Who has 7:10?

••• I have

Who has 9:35?

I have

Who has 3:05?

I have

Who has 3:35?

I have

Who has 1:25?

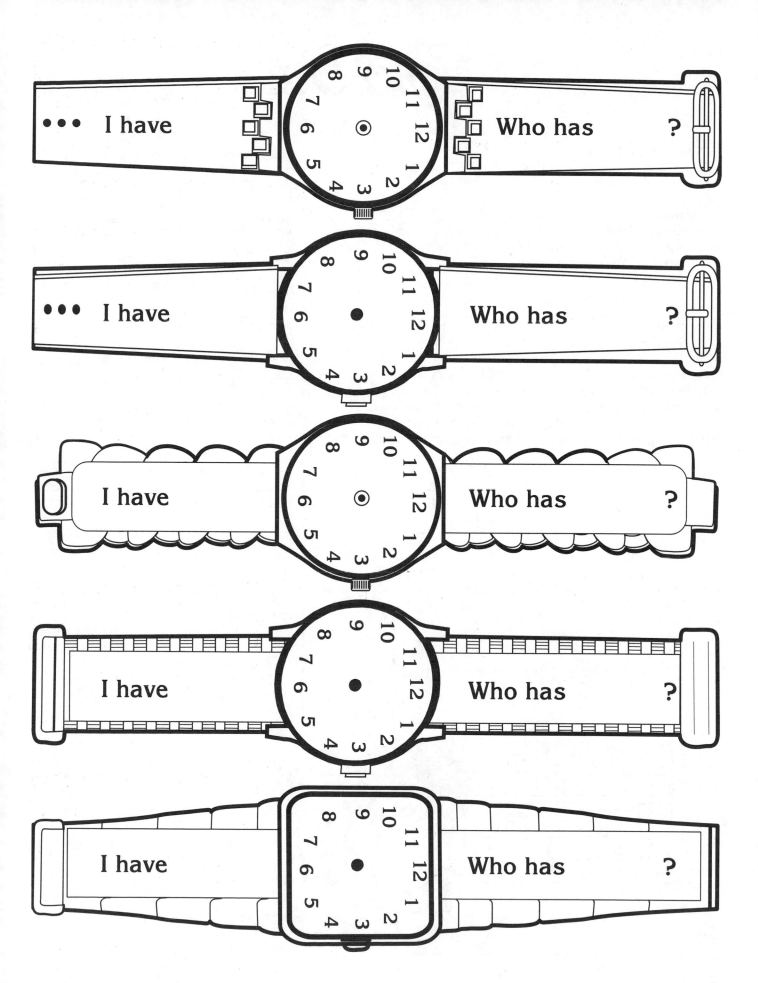

Time Out

Object of the Game

To have four boxes in a row, column, or diagonal covered with chips.

Materials

For each student:
    one *Time Out* game board (see *Management 1*)
    covering chips (see *Management 1*)
    glue
    scissors

For the class:
    set of *Time Out Clue Cards* (see *Management 3*)

Management

1. For each child to make his or her own *Time Out* game board, copy several sets of the time cards, and allow each student to choose 16 time cards to cut out and glue onto their own bingo grid.

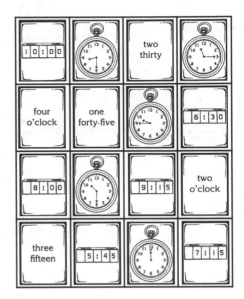

2. Each student will need 16 chips to cover the game board. Beans, math chips, bingo chips and even small squares of paper will work.
3. The *Time Out Clue Cards* can be copied on card stock, cut out, and laminated for extended use or read directly from the page.

Procedure

1. Give a game board and 16 chips to each student. Talk about and demonstrate the game's objective.
2. Explain that you have a set of clue cards that have different times on them. Tell the students that you will choose a card and will read the time out loud. They are to look for that time on their game board in digital, analog, or word notation. If they have the chosen time, they are to cover its space. When they have four boxes covered in a row, column, or diagonal, they are to call "time out."
3. Have the student that called "time out" tell which boxes were covered. Check to make sure the answers are correct.

Time Out

12:00	12:15	12:30	12:45
11:00	11:15	11:30	11:45
10:00	10:15	10:30	10:45
9:00	9:15	9:30	9:45
8:00	8:15	8:30	8:45
7:00	7:15	7:30	7:45

Time Out

6:00	6:15	6:30	6:45
5:00	5:15	5:30	5:45
4:00	4:15	4:30	4:45
3:00	3:15	3:30	3:45
2:00	2:15	2:30	2:45
1:00	1:15	1:30	1:45

twelve o'clock	twelve fifteen	twelve thirty	twelve forty-five
eleven o'clock	eleven fifteen	eleven thirty	eleven forty-five
ten o'clock	ten fifteen	ten thirty	ten forty-five
nine o'clock	nine fifteen	nine thirty	nine forty-five

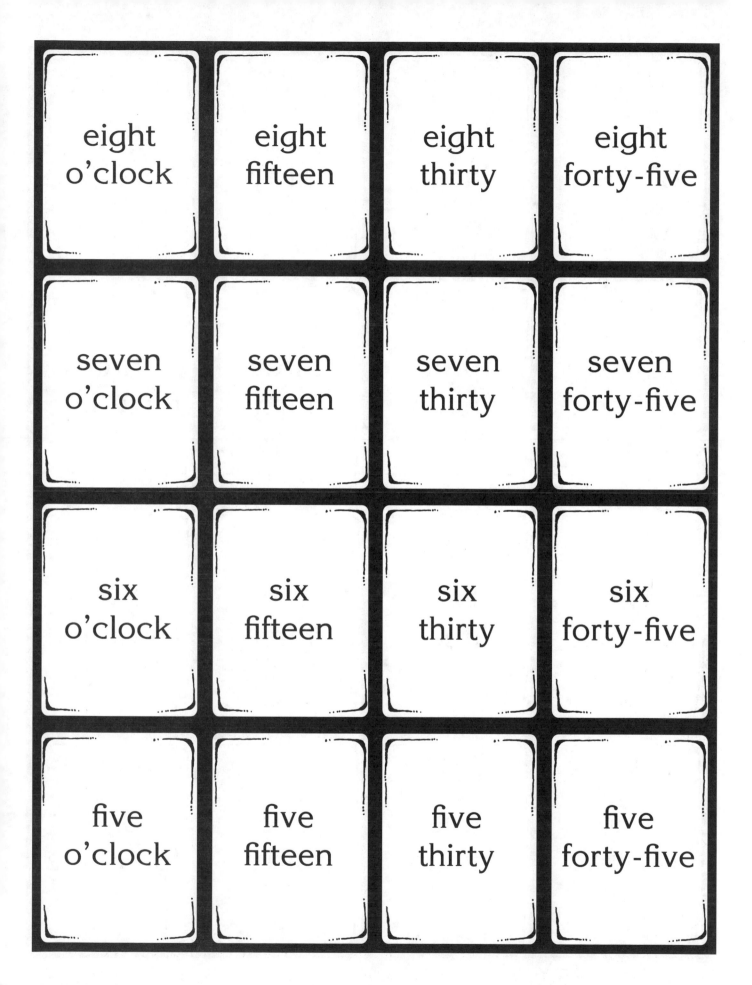

eight o'clock	eight fifteen	eight thirty	eight forty-five
seven o'clock	seven fifteen	seven thirty	seven forty-five
six o'clock	six fifteen	six thirty	six forty-five
five o'clock	five fifteen	five thirty	five forty-five

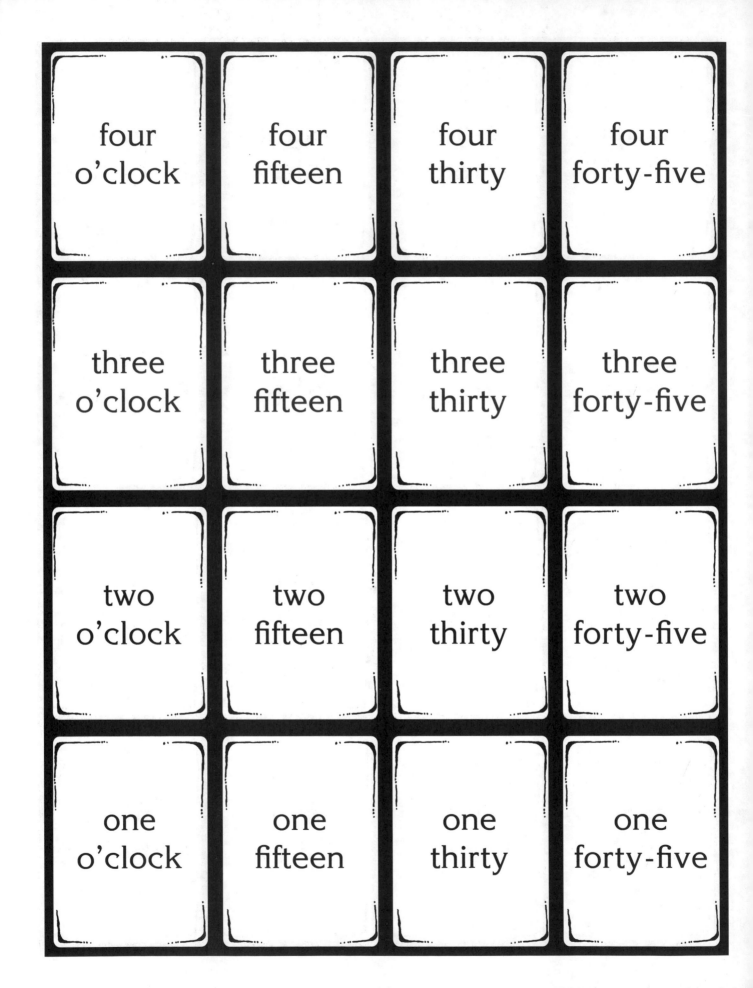

four o'clock	four fifteen	four thirty	four forty-five
three o'clock	three fifteen	three thirty	three forty-five
two o'clock	two fifteen	two thirty	two forty-five
one o'clock	one fifteen	one thirty	one forty-five

The AIMS Program

AIMS is the acronym for "Activities Integrating Mathematics and Science." Such integration enriches learning and makes it meaningful and holistic. AIMS began as a project of Fresno Pacific University to integrate the study of mathematics and science in grades K-9, but has since expanded to include language arts, social studies, and other disciplines.

AIMS is a continuing program of the non-profit AIMS Education Foundation. It had its inception in a National Science Foundation funded program whose purpose was to explore the effectiveness of integrating mathematics and science. The project directors in cooperation with 80 elementary classroom teachers devoted two years to a thorough field-testing of the results and implications of integration.

The approach met with such positive results that the decision was made to launch a program to create instructional materials incorporating this concept. Despite the fact that thoughtful educators have long recommended an integrative approach, very little appropriate material was available in 1981 when the project began. A series of writing projects have ensued and today the AIMS Education Foundation is committed to continue the creation of new integrated activities on a permanent basis.

The AIMS program is funded through the sale of this developing series of books and proceeds from the Foundation's endowment. All net income from program and products flows into a trust fund administered by the AIMS Education Foundation. Use of these funds is restricted to support of research, development, and publication of new materials. Writers donate all their rights to the Foundation to support its on-going program. No royalties are paid to the writers.

The rationale for integration lies in the fact that science, mathematics, language arts, social studies, etc., are integrally interwoven in the real world from which it follows that they should be similarly treated in the classroom where we are preparing students to live in that world. Teachers who use the AIMS program give enthusiastic endorsement to the effectiveness of this approach.

Science encompasses the art of questioning, investigating, hypothesizing, discovering, and communicating. Mathematics is a language that provides clarity, objectivity, and understanding. The language arts provide us powerful tools of communication. Many of the major contemporary societal issues stem from advancements in science and must be studied in the context of the social sciences. Therefore, it is timely that all of us take seriously a more holistic mode of educating our students. This goal motivates all who are associated with the AIMS Program. We invite you to join us in this effort.

Meaningful integration of knowledge is a major recommendation coming from the nation's professional science and mathematics associations. The American Association for the Advancement of Science in *Science for All Americans* strongly recommends the integration of mathematics, science, and technology. The National Council of Teachers of Mathematics places strong emphasis on applications of mathematics such as are found in science investigations. AIMS is fully aligned with these recommendations.

Extensive field testing of AIMS investigations confirms these beneficial results.

1. Mathematics becomes more meaningful, hence more useful, when it is applied to situations that interest students.
2. The extent to which science is studied and understood is increased, with a significant economy of time, when mathematics and science are integrated.
3. There is improved quality of learning and retention, supporting the thesis that learning which is meaningful and relevant is more effective.
4. Motivation and involvement are increased dramatically as students investigate real-world situations and participate actively in the process.
   We invite you to become part of this classroom teacher movement by using an integrated approach to learning and sharing any suggestions you may have. The AIMS Program welcomes you!

AIMS Education Foundation Programs

A Day with AIMS®

Intensive one-day workshops are offered to introduce educators to the philosophy and rationale of AIMS. Participants will discuss the methodology of AIMS and the strategies by which AIMS principles may be incorporated into curriculum. Each participant will take part in a variety of hands-on AIMS investigations to gain an understanding of such aspects as the scientific/mathematical content, classroom management, and connections with other curricular areas. *A Day with AIMS®* workshops may be offered anywhere in the United States. Necessary supplies and take-home materials are usually included in the enrollment fee.

A Week with AIMS®

Throughout the nation, AIMS offers many one-week workshops each year, usually in the summer. Each workshop lasts five days and includes at least 30 hours of AIMS hands-on instruction. Participants are grouped according to the grade level(s) in which they are interested. Instructors are members of the AIMS Instructional Leadership Network. Supplies for the activities and a generous supply of take-home materials are included in the enrollment fee. Sites are selected on the basis of applications submitted by educational organizations. If chosen to host a workshop, the host agency agrees to provide specified facilities and cooperate in the promotion of the workshop. The AIMS Education Foundation supplies workshop materials as well as the travel, housing, and meals for instructors.

AIMS One-Week Perspectives Workshops

Each summer, Fresno Pacific University offers AIMS one-week workshops on its campus in Fresno, California. AIMS Program Directors and highly qualified members of the AIMS National Leadership Network serve as instructors.

The AIMS Instructional Leadership Program

This is an AIMS staff-development program seeking to prepare facilitators for leadership roles in science/math education in their home districts or regions. Upon successful completion of the program, trained facilitators may become members of the AIMS Instructional Leadership Network, qualified to conduct AIMS workshops, teach AIMS in-service courses for college credit, and serve as AIMS consultants. Intensive training is provided in mathematics, science, process and thinking skills, workshop management, and other relevant topics.

College Credit and Grants

Those who participate in workshops may often qualify for college credit. If the workshop takes place on the campus of Fresno Pacific University, that institution may grant appropriate credit. If the workshop takes place off-campus, arrangements can sometimes be made for credit to be granted by another institution. In addition, the applicant's home school district is often willing to grant in-service or professional-development credit. Many educators who participate in AIMS workshops are recipients of various types of educational grants, either local or national. Nationally known foundations and funding agencies have long recognized the value of AIMS mathematics and science workshops to educators. The AIMS Education Foundation encourages educators interested in attending or hosting workshops to explore the pos-sibilities suggested above. Although the Foundation strongly supports such interest, it reminds applicants that they have the primary responsibility for fulfilling *current* requirements.

For current information regarding the programs described above, please complete the following:

Information Request

Please send current information on the items checked:

____ *Basic Information Packet* on AIMS materials	____ *A Week with AIMS®* workshops
____ *AIMS Instructional Leadership Program*	____ Hosting information for *A Day with AIMS®* workshops
____ *AIMS One-Week Perspectives* workshops	____ Hosting information for *A Week with AIMS®* workshops

Name _____   Phone _____

Address _____
      Street   City   State   Zip

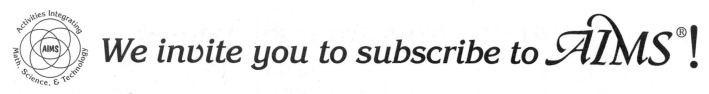

We invite you to subscribe to *AIMS*®!

Each issue of *AIMS*® contains a variety of material useful to educators at all grade levels. Feature articles of lasting value deal with topics such as mathematical or science concepts, curriculum, assessment, the teaching of process skills, and historical background. Several of the latest AIMS math/science investigations are always included, along with their reproducible activity sheets. As needs direct and space allows, various issues contain news of current developments, such as workshop schedules, activities of the AIMS Instructional Leadership Network, and announcements of upcoming publications.

AIMS® is published monthly, August through May. Subscriptions are on an annual basis only. A subscription entered at any time will begin with the next issue, but will also include the previous issues of that volume. Readers have preferred this arrangement because articles and activities within an annual volume are often interrelated.

Please note that an *AIMS*® subscription automatically includes duplication rights for one school site for all issues included in the subscription. Many schools build cost-effective library resources with their subscriptions.

YES! I am interested in subscribing to *AIMS*®.

Name _____ Home Phone _____

Address _____ City, State, Zip _____

Please send the following volumes (subject to availability):

_____	Volume	VII	(1992-93)	$15.00	_____	Volume	XII	(1997-98)	$30.00
_____	Volume	VIII	(1993-94)	$15.00	_____	Volume	XIII	(1998-99)	$30.00
_____	Volume	IX	(1994-95)	$15.00	_____	Volume	XIV	(1999-00)	$30.00
_____	Volume	X	(1995-96)	$15.00	_____	Volume	XV	(2000-01)	$30.00
_____	Volume	XI	(1996-97)	$30.00	_____	Volume	XVI	(2001-02)	$30.00

_____**Limited offer: Volumes XVI & XVII (2001-2003) $55.00**

(Note: Prices may change without notice)

Check your method of payment:

☐ Check enclosed in the amount of $_____

☐ Purchase order attached (Please include the P.O.#, the authorizing signature, and position of the authorizing person.)

☐ Credit Card ☐ Visa ☐ MasterCard Amount $ _____

Card # _____ Expiration Date _____

Signature _____ Today's Date _____

Make checks payable to **AIMS Education Foundation.**
Mail to *AIMS*® Magazine, P.O. Box 8120, Fresno, CA 93747-8120.
Phone (559) 255-4094 or (888) 733-2467 FAX (559) 255-6396
AIMS Homepage: http://www.AIMSedu.org/

AIMS Program Publications

Actions with Fractions 4-9
Bats Incredible! 2-4
Brick Layers 4-9
Brick Layers II 4-9
Cycles of Knowing and Growing 1-3
Crazy about Cotton Book 3-7
Critters K-6
Down to Earth 5-9
Electrical Connections 4-9
Exploring Environments Book K-6
Fabulous Fractions 3-6
Fall into Math and Science K-1
Field Detectives 3-6
Finding Your Bearings 4-9
Floaters and Sinkers 5-9
From Head to Toe 5-9
Fun with Foods 5-9
Glide into Winter with Math & Science K-1
Gravity Rules! Activity Book 5-12
Hardhatting in a Geo-World 3-5
It's About Time K-2
Jaw Breakers and Heart Thumpers 3-5
Just for the Fun of It! 4-9
Looking at Lines 6-9
Machine Shop 5-9
Magnificent Microworld Adventures 5-9
Math + Science, A Solution 5-9
Mostly Magnets 2-8
Multiplication the Algebra Way 4-8
Off The Wall Science 3-9
Our Wonderful World 5-9
Out of This World 4-8
Overhead and Underfoot 3-5
Paper Square Geometry:
    The Mathematics of Origami
Puzzle Play: 4-8
Pieces and Patterns 5-9
Popping With Power 3-5
Primarily Bears K-6
Primarily Earth K-3

Primarily Physics K-3
Primarily Plants K-3
Proportional Reasoning 6-9
Ray's Reflections 4-8
Sense-Able Science K-1
Soap Films and Bubbles 4-9
Spatial Visualization 4-9
Spills and Ripples 5-12
Spring into Math and Science K-1
The Amazing Circle 4-9
The Budding Botanist 3-6
The Sky's the Limit 5-9
Through the Eyes of the Explorers 5-9
Under Construction K-2
Water Precious Water 2-6
Weather Sense:
    Temperature, Air Pressure, and Wind 4-5
Winter Wonders K-2

Spanish/English Editions
Brinca de alegria hacia la Primavera con las
    Matemáticas y Ciencias K-1
Cáete de gusto hacia el Otoño con las
    Matemáticas y Ciencias K-1
Conexiones Eléctricas 4-9
El Botanista Principiante 3-6
Los Cinco Sentidos K-1
Ositos Nada Más K-6
Patine al Invierno con Matemáticas y Ciencias K-1
Piezas y Diseños 5-9
Primariamente Física K-3
Primariamente Plantas K-3
Principalmente Imanes 2-8

All Spanish/English Editions include student pages in
Spanish and teacher and student pages in English.

Spanish Edition
Constructores II: Ingeniería Creativa Con Construcciones LEGO® (4-9)
The entire book is written in Spanish. English pages not included.

Other Science and Math Publications
Historical Connections in Mathematics, Vol. I 5-9
Historical Connections in Mathematics, Vol. II 5-9
Historical Connections in Mathematics, Vol. III 5-9
Mathematicians are People, Too
Mathematicians are People, Too, Vol. II
Teaching Science with Everyday Things
What's Next, Volume 1, 4-12
What's Next, Volume 2, 4-12
What's Next, Volume 3, 4-12

For further information write to:
AIMS Education Foundation • P.O. Box 8120 • Fresno, California 93747-8120
www.AIMSedu.org/ • Fax 559•255•6396

AIMS Duplication Rights Program

AIMS has received many requests from school districts for the purchase of unlimited duplication rights to AIMS materials. In response, the AIMS Education Foundation has formulated the program outlined below. There is a built-in flexibility which, we trust, will provide for those who use AIMS materials extensively to purchase such rights for either individual activities or entire books.

It is the goal of the AIMS Education Foundation to make its materials and programs available at reasonable cost. All income from the sale of publications and duplication rights is used to support AIMS programs; hence, strict adherence to regulations governing duplication is essential. Duplication of AIMS materials beyond limits set by copyright laws and those specified below is strictly forbidden.

Limited Duplication Rights

Any purchaser of an AIMS book may make up to *200 copies* of any activity in that book for use at *one school site*. Beyond that, rights must be purchased according to the appropriate category.

Unlimited Duplication Rights for Single Activities

An individual or school may purchase the right to make an unlimited number of copies of a single activity. The royalty is $5.00 per activity per school site.

Examples: 3 activities x 1 site x $5.00 = $15.00
9 activities x 3 sites x $5.00 = $135.00

Unlimited Duplication Rights for Entire Books

A school or district may purchase the right to make an unlimited number of copies of a single, *specified* book. The royalty is $20.00 per book per school site. This is in addition to the cost of the book.

Examples: 5 books x 1 site x $20.00 = $100.00
12 books x 10 sites x $20.00 = $2400.00

Magazine/Newsletter Duplication Rights

Those who purchase *AIMS*® (magazine)/*Newsletter* are hereby granted permission to make up to 200 copies of any portion of it, provided these copies will be used for educational purposes.

Workshop Instructors' Duplication Rights

Workshop instructors may distribute to registered workshop participants a maximum of 100 copies of any article and/or 100 copies of no more than eight activities, provided these six conditions are met:

1. Since all AIMS activities are based upon the *AIMS Model of Mathematics* and the *AIMS Model of Learning*, leaders must include in their presentations an explanation of these two models.
2. Workshop instructors must relate the AIMS activities presented to these basic explanations of the AIMS philosophy of education.
3. The copyright notice must appear on all materials distributed.
4. Instructors must provide information enabling participants to order books and magazines from the Foundation.
5. Instructors must inform participants of their limited duplication rights as outlined below.
6. Only student pages may be duplicated.

Written permission must be obtained for duplication beyond the limits listed above. Additional royalty payments may be required.

Workshop Participants' Rights

Those enrolled in workshops in which AIMS student activity sheets are distributed may duplicate a maximum of 35 copies or enough to use the lessons one time with one class, whichever is less. Beyond that, rights must be purchased according to the appropriate category.

Application for Duplication Rights

The purchasing agency or individual must clearly specify the following:
1. Name, address, and telephone number
2. Titles of the books for Unlimited Duplication Rights contracts
3. Titles of activities for Unlimited Duplication Rights contracts
4. Names and addresses of school sites for which duplication rights are being purchased.

NOTE: Books to be duplicated must be purchased separately and are not included in the contract for Unlimited Duplication Rights.

The requested duplication rights are automatically authorized when proper payment is received, although a *Certificate of Duplication Rights* will be issued when the application is processed.

Address all correspondence to: **Contract Division**
AIMS Education Foundation   www.AIMSedu.org/
P.O. Box 8120   Fax 559•255•6396
Fresno, CA 93747-8120